CW00348364

THE MONASTIC INSTITUTES

John Cassian,
Abbot of Marseilles

THE MONASTIC INSTITUTES

consisting of

ON THE TRAINING OF A MONK

and

THE EIGHT DEADLY SINS

In Twelve Books

Translated by Father Jerome Bertram
of the Oxford Oratory

The Saint Austin Press
MCMXCIX

THE SAINT AUSTIN PRESS
296 Brockley Road
London   SE4 2RA
Tel   +44 (0) 181 692 6009
Fax +44 (0) 181 469 3609

Email: books@saintaustin.org
http://www.saintaustin.org

A catalogue record for this book is available from the British Library.

ISBN 1 901157 04 0

NIHIL OBSTAT:
The Reverend Michael Clifton
IMPRIMATUR:
The Reverend Canon Mgr. John Hine VG
Westminster, 25th November 1998

The Nihil obstat *and* Imprimatur *are a declaration that a book is considered to be freee from doctrinal or moral error. It is not implied that those who have granted the* Nihil obstat *and* Imprimatur *agree with the contents, opinions statements expressed*

Contents

Translator's Introduction
John Cassian
a Spiritual Guide for the Laity

Lay people today, both in the Church and outside it, are eager for spiritual guidance, longing to develop a life of prayer, and ready to listen to almost anyone who offers a path to holiness. Teachers from many exotic cultures, both sound and dubious, are sure of an audience. Yet the spiritual traditions of the West have been almost lost to sight, for reasons which still remain unclear. This version of Cassian, who influenced Western spirituality more than most, is offered as a help and guide for those in our modern world who are still struggling against the ancient problems of life, and who yearn for a deeper union with God. Cassian's name is not familiar, indeed if he is remembered at all, he is usually considered a monk's writer, a voice from the remote past speaking to men of terrifying asceticism who lived far apart from the hurly-burly of everyday life. Monks, it used to be safely assumed, can all read Latin with ease, and therefore no translation of this ancient writer is necessary, save for those few academics who still concern themselves with such matters.

Presenting Cassian to the laity may therefore seem rather perverse - but there is good precedent. The teaching of Cassian, although unacknowledged, underlies the spirituality of St Philip Neri and St Francis de Sales, both of whom dedicated themselves to the sanctification of the lay state, teaching methods of prayer suitable for men and women in different states of life, both busy and leisured. Theirs is not the only Western spiritual tradition available for the laity - indeed the teaching of the Jesuits is far better known and widely practised - but it is one which certainly suits many people who find St Ignatius rather difficult.

There is a celebrated passage in Newman's Oratory papers where he contrasts the two spiritualities, comparing the Oratorian tradition of St Philip and St Francis de Sales to the Athenians, and the Jesuit tradition to the Spartans as described by Pericles in his Funeral Speech. (*Newman the Oratorian*, ed. Placid Murray, pp 210-2) The comparison may not spring immediately to mind in our post-Classical age, but the distinction between two grand streams of spiritual teaching is, I believe, valid, and could usefully be explored further. Both traditions are authentic, both are necessary to the life of the Church, but those who are happy with a writer, an Order or a spiritual director of one tradition will find themselves quite ill at ease when confronted with one from the other tradition.

Newman went further, and suggested that an Oratorian is "almost the reverse ... of a Jesuit." (*ibid.* p. 208) He was not only thinking of the very different structures, the Society of Jesus being centrally organised and governed from above, whereas the Oratory is so democratic as to be almost anarchical, but also of that much more intangible quality, the approach to prayer, and to the teaching of prayer. Here the Oratory finds itself in a natural association with the older Orders, with the Benedictines, the Dominicans and the Carmelites. Abbot John Chapman's teaching on prayer, with his famous dictum "Pray as you can and don't try to pray as you can't", epitomises our approach. (See his *Spiritual Letters*) Prayer is unstructured, chaotic perhaps, free, without rigid method or set forms, but is none the less diligently practised and regularly observed. Prayer is infinitely adaptable, for the different circumstances in which we find ourselves. Our prayer and our whole way of life are marked by a lightness of touch which prevents us from ever taking ourselves too seriously.

There is an "Athenian" approach also to the pursuit of virtue. Sin, also, must not be taken too seriously, for that would be to play straight into its clutches. The devil cannot abide being laughed at, as C.S. Lewis has shown us, and a breezy confidence in the effective grace of God may do more to dispel the darkness of vice than intent and gloomy dwellings on the minutiae of sin. Vice can be seen as a disease, a virus, a poison which we are trying to expel from our system, or it may be seen as a sporting challenge to be surpassed, and the approach to treating this disease or meeting this challenge can be one of cheerful confidence once we have embarked on a programme of spiritual life.

I am not going to attempt to describe exactly what the difference between the two types of spirituality is, for it is essentially something that can only be grasped from much reading and much experience. But perhaps I may suggest that "Athenians" will be those who feel at home, not only with Abbot Chapman and St Francis de Sales but with the mediaeval English mystics, the *Cloud*, Hilton, Rolle, and their eccentric follower Austin Baker, with Aelred of Rievaulx and Bernard of Clairvaulx, William of St Thierry and the Victorines, and further back, with Denis the Areopagite, and hence with his sixteenth-century follower John of the Cross, and the formidable Teresa of Avila. "Athenians" will recognise that the only clear rule you can really give on prayer is St Benedict's concise "If you want to pray, just go into the Oratory and pray." (*Rule*, chapter 52) And behind all these teachers on prayer will be found the giant figure of John Cassian.

So who was Cassian? For his life and a discussion of his works we cannot do better than refer to Owen Chadwick's *John Cassian* (1950, 2nd edition 1968). The theological problems of grace raised by the charge of "Semi-Pelagianism" are too complex to be attempted in a short introduction, though perhaps one day we may attempt a scholarly edition with full commentary and notes. For the present we may be content with a brief summary. John Cassian came either from the Danube Delta or from Provence, and must have been quite young when he entered a monastery in Bethlehem in or before the year 382. After a few years of formation in community he and a close friend called Germanus gained permission to visit the monasteries of Egypt, inspired by their contact with the fugitive Abba Pinufius (see Book IV, chapter 31). They seem to have reached Egypt in about 385, stayed seven years, visited Bethlehem briefly to be released from their obligation to that community, and returned to Egypt where they lived until the crisis of 399.

This crisis was the bringing to a head of the rivalry between the simpler Coptic-speaking native monks and the more sophisticated Greek-speakers. The Egyptians accused the Greeks of "Origenism" while the Greeks retaliated with a charge of "Anthropomorphism." The upshot was a general exodus of Greeks, including Cassian and Germanus, who came to Constantinople where they met and admired St John Chrysostom. Similarities in approach between the two writers are obvious, and Chrysostom's great outburst in praise of the monastic life in his commentary on I Timothy could well owe something to Cassian's stories of what he saw in Egypt. (Homily XIV, in *Library of the Fathers* Vol. 12, 1843, pp 122-5) Cassian was ordained deacon by Chrysostom, but on the latter's fall from favour at court and exile, had to leave Constantinople in 403. He passed through Rome, and settled finally at Marseilles where he was ordained priest and founded two monasteries, for women and for men, the latter dedicated to St Victor. Here he lived at peace, for Provence escaped the turbulence which swept over Italy in the early fifth century, and here he died in 435.

Cassian's three surviving books, and the only ones he is known to have written, seem all to date from between 425 and 430. The occasion for the first, the *Institutes,* was an appeal from Castor, bishop of Apt, for help and advice in founding a monastery. It is clear that the *Institutes* and the *Collations* or *Conferences* were being written at the same time, from frequent cross-references. The *Institutes* present a systematic treatise on how to be a monk, and how to grow in virtue and combat vice, whereas the *Collations* are reports of conversations between the young monks Cassian and Germanus, and the various elders of Egypt. The third, more theological, treatise *De Incarnatione* was an answer to the Nestorian crisis of 429-31, and on quite a different level from the monastic writings.

In describing Egyptian or Palestinian monasticism, and recommending practical modifications for Provence, Cassian is clearly not reporting verbatim conversations he heard thirty or forty years before: in the Preface to the *Institutes* he admits as much. What we find here are his mature deliberations, drawing on the experience of many years in different sorts of monasteries, although certainly profoundly influenced by what he and Germanus saw and heard during their time in Egypt. Chadwick has pointed out how the scheme of eight deadly sins owes much to the now discredited Evagrius, who really was an Origenist and who wrote in Egypt shortly before Cassian's time. Discussion over the text, and the degree to which we can detect interpolations or rearrangements could be endless; substantially we can say that the text we have is authentic, although a few chapters may be out of place. Again I would refer the reader to Chadwick for further illumination.

Cassian, as is well known, was St Benedict's primary acknowledged authority on monasticism. In fact we find the Father of Monks recommending Cassian for daily reading. (*Rule,* chapter 42) This reading often took place while the monks took a little light refreshment. Cassian's major work the *Collations* thus gave a name to breakfast in a number of European languages (Italian *collazione,* Polish *kolacja* and so on), an indication of how widespread his influence became. St Dominic also recommended Cassian for daily reading, but it was our own St Philip Neri who first dared to read Cassian to laypeople, to men of the world, to young men in the process of discerning their vocation or deciding on a career. When the "Exercises of the Oratory" were first begun in Rome, as often as not Philip would have a page of Cassian read as a text on which to comment for the benefit of his young lay audience.

St Philip died in 1595, and Cassian remained a popular author for a few years more, judging by the number of editions printed, but after Gazet's great commentary on Cassian had passed through its second edition in 1628, (*Ioannis Cassiani opera omnia cum commentariis D. Alardi Gazaei,* Arras, 1628) something of an eclipse seems to have come over our author. A different spirituality dominated the Church, and Cassian was out of favour. Perhaps the most striking instance of this is seen in the reaction of St Alphonsus (a "Spartan" if ever there was one) when he caught one of his priests reading Cassian - "I would prefer to see your Reverence study my book on moral theology for half-an-hour a day ... rather than hear that you are studying Cassian." (Frederick M. Jones, *Alphonsus de Liguori,* p. 318)

Cassian's descent into obscurity must be the explanation of why such a seminal author has never been completely translated into English. His works were reissued twice in Latin during the nineteenth century: Migne in the *Patrologia Latina* vols. 49-50 simply reprinted Gazet's edition, making a few new mistakes and inserting some inaccurate Biblical references. A far better edition appeared in the Viennese series, *Corpus Scriptorum Ecclesiasticorum Latinorum* (vols 13 and 17, edited by Michael Petschenig, 1886 and 1888) which is the basis of our translation. A monk of Mount St Bernard translated most of the *Collations* under their more familiar title of *Conferences* in a little undated edition, probably about 1860, of such rarity that the Bodleian Library does not possess a copy. (*Cassian's Conferences freely translated,* by Father Robert of Mount St Bernard's Abbey, 2 vols., London, n.d.) Small selections of the *Conferences* have more recently appeared in the *Library of Christian Classics,* (Vol XII, London 1958), and the *Classics of Western Spirituality,* (with an introduction by Owen Chadwick, New York / Mahwah 1985). The only translation which purports to include all Cassian's works is that by Edgar C.S. Gibson in Vol XI of the *Nicene and Post-Nicene Fathers,* (Oxford & New York, 1894, reprinted Grand Rapids 1964), but we find in this that three whole books have been omitted, namely Book VI of the *Institutes* and Books XII and XXII of the *Collations.*

The omission of these books neatly makes my point about the two spiritualities: the "Athenian" spirituality of Cassian can talk quite frankly about sexual sin, point out some practical suggestions for breaking bad habits, and encourage us to defuse the situation by cheerfully recognising that chastity is a gift from God which will be granted once we stop worrying about it and accept that we cannot reform ourselves by sheer will power. The "Spartan" spirituality would rather not talk about it, but assumes that you have dealt with that problem on your own before you venture to sully the church with your presence. Cassian tells us that a sexual bad habit can usually be expected to disappear after about six months in the monastery; the more recent tradition was to demand six months' perfect purity before even beginning the monastic life.

The gaps in Gibson's translation were made up by Terrence Kardong in *Cassian on Chastity* (Assumption Abbey Press 1993), but it is still true that no complete unabridged English translation of one of the most important masters of the spiritual life has ever been available. The present version of the *Institutes* is the first stage in supplying a version for popular reading, to be followed, if God gives us grace (as Cassian would say), by the *Collations* and the *Incarnation*. Our intention is to make Cassian accessible for the modern reader, offered for the first time since St Philip's days to laypeople who are striving to live the Christian life, as well as for monks and similar professionals. For as I said, St Philip has shown us that Cassian's writings are profitable for people in all walks of life, and can be a valuable asset in the task of sanctifying the lay state which was St Philip's special concern.

The *Institutes* must therefore be read with a measure of flexibility and common sense. Clearly not everything here is going to be useful for the lay reader, or even for the monk. If I might make a suggestion, I would recommend that in a first reading you omit the first three books altogether. There is something useful to be gained in Cassian's comments on the monastic habit (not the least being the recognition that a special habit was part of monastic life from the very beginning) and there are nuggets of gold in the apparently dry sections on the night and day psalms, but the fourth book is probably the first one of general interest, and for many readers the second part of the work, on the Eight Deadly Sins, will be far more useful than anything in the first part.

It will be seen that Cassian's list only partly overlaps with St Gregory's better known set of seven sins, but perhaps we need to mention again that he treats the vices as diseases or challenges, not as malicious acts. As we struggle against one bad tendency or another, it is heartening to be reassured that we are not alone, that the great saints and heroes of the early centuries recognised in themselves the same human failings, and have left us sage advice as we follow in their footsteps. Cassian uses two metaphors throughout his treatment of the sins: one is that of the doctor applying appropriate precautions and medicines in treating his patient, where the emphasis is on the healing ministry of the spiritual director. The other lays more stress on the struggling soul, seen in the metaphor of an athlete competing in the highly organised professional Greek games, in what we may call an "Octathlon." The eight sins must be tackled one after another, and in the right order, just as the athlete has to compete in different events, qualifying in one so that he may present himself for the next.

In presenting Cassian for the modern reader I am not merely making available a historical document, but offering what I hope will be something useful in the conduct of our daily life. With this purpose of sustaining the spirituality of the laity, then, I venture to dedicate this translation to the Brothers of the Little Oratory in Oxford.

JFAB, September 1997

ON THE TRAINING OF A MONK

Preface, Addressed to Pope Castor

The Old Testament histories tell us that Solomon, the wisest of men, was granted by God a great measure of wisdom and discernment from God, as well as a broadness of understanding, infinite as the sands of the sea (*I Kings 4:29*), so that, as God's word testifies, no one like him had ever existed in previous ages, nor would be found after him. He in return was eager to build a magnificent Temple for the Lord, and asked for the assistance of the King of Tyre, a foreigner. When Hiram, the son of a widow, was sent to him, Solomon was able to draw on his advice and expertise to carry out the things that his divine wisdom had suggested to him for the enhancement of the Temple of the Lord, and its sacred vessels. (*I Kings 5*) Now therefore, if the greatest prince of all the realms on earth, the offspring of the noblest and finest stock of Israel, one so inspired by the wisdom of God as to surpass all the learning and skills of the East and of Egypt, was not ashamed to ask advice of a poor man who was a foreigner, you are quite justified in following his example, most blessed Pope Castor. For you have determined to construct a true and reasonable temple for God, not built of unfeeling stones but by gathering men of holiness, a temple which will not pass away or decay, but will remain for ever incorruptible. You have been anxious to consecrate precious vessels to the Lord, not beaten out of dumb gold and silver like those which the King of Babel plundered and handed over to his debauched women and followers (*Dan. 5*) but moulded out of the souls of the holy, glittering with innocence, honesty and purity, and bearing Christ their King around within themselves. And you have not hesitated to call on me to help with this work, me who am poor and in every way inadequate!

There are as yet no monasteries in your diocese, but you have determined to make a foundation on the Egyptian or Oriental model.

3

I know that you have already advanced far in grace and knowledge, and are experienced in spirituality, so that not only your preaching but your very way of life is a good guide for those who seek perfection, and you have invited me, one quite unskilled in preaching and knowledge, to contribute something towards your project out of my inadequacy. You asked me to describe to the brothers of your new monastery the monastic customs which we saw in action in Egypt and Palestine, and which the fathers there explained to us. I may be unskilled in fine writing, but you are not asking for eloquent prose (which you could write far better than I) but a simple description of the simple life of the saints. I am fired by your wishes to carry them out, but equally daunted by the greatness of the undertaking. To begin with, my own life has not prepared me to undertake to describe such difficult, obscure and indeed sublime matters. And then it is many years since, in my youth, I and my companion lived among the Fathers and learned from them, were instructed by their daily preaching and example and even attempted to imitate them. What they taught us, and what we observed of them, I can hardly claim to remember now in full, for it is so long since we left their company and their example. Moreover these matters of their nature cannot be adequately treated in casual conversation, neither taught nor learnt simply in words, nor can they be kept in the memory - monasticism is essentially a life to be lived. Only those who have experienced this life can pass it on, and only those who have imitated it with equal care and effort can understand it or comprehend it. The subject needs to be discussed earnestly with spiritual men, and kept fresh, lest it slip away from the careless memory. And then again, since I am liable to remember not so much what is most important in itself, but what seems most relevant to the moment, my description will fall short of a proper account.

Besides all this, writers of exemplary life, skilled in conveying their knowledge, have already written much on the subject – men like St Basil and St Jerome among others. Basil gave clear answers, well backed by Scripture quotations, to the eager questions of his monks

THE MONASTIC INSTITUTES

about different customs and points of enquiry; Jerome not only wrote books out of his own considerable experience, but also translated Greek works and put them into elegant Latin. After such floods of lucid rhetoric, I would rightly be considered impertinent if I attempted to add my own trickle. Only the confidence I gain from Your Holiness can reassure me, with the guarantee that these trifles will be in some way pleasing to you; and at least you can commend them to the brothers who live in your new monastery.

I can trust these brothers to read my inexpert fumblings devoutly and with compassionate tolerance, for they will be more interested in the sense than in the style. Therefore, most Holy Father, model of piety and modesty, I am inspired by your prayers to attempt the task you have set me to the best of my ability, and since those who have written before me have completely omitted some matters, as if they were trying to describe what they had heard of rather than what they had experienced, I will describe them for the benefit of a new community, eager for knowledge. I shall not be concerned to weave in stories of miracles and portents, although the elders did tell us many incredible things, and we actually witnessed such things happening in our presence: nevertheless I shall omit all these, since they would only move the readers to wonder, rather than to improve their life. I shall merely describe the customs and rules of the monasteries.

In particular I shall attempt to describe faithfully the origins and causes of the principal vices, which they reckon to be eight in number, and the usual means of curing them, as far as the Lord shall give me the ability. My plan is not so much to talk about the wonders of God, but to say something on the improvement of our way of life and the attaining of perfection according to what the elders told us. I shall endeavour to satisfy your request, that I shall make recommendations either for or against the adoption in our diocese of any point which depends on the whim of a particular monastic founder, rather than the oldest tradition and opinion of the majority, but I shall do so on the authority of what seems to be the rule and authentic tradition of the monasteries which were first founded in Egypt or Palestine. You

5

could not design a more sensible or ideal rule for a new foundation in the western region of Gaul than those customs which have survived to our own time from the first preaching of the Apostles in monasteries founded by holy and spiritual fathers. However I shall be so bold as to introduce into this work some moderation of the original Egyptian rule, which I deem too harsh and impossible in these parts, because of the coldness of the climate or for sheer difficulty or strangeness – this I shall temper slightly with the customs of monasteries in Palestine or Mesopotamia, since if we keep to a sensible measure of what is feasible, perfection will be found in observing it, even for those of weak ability.

BOOK ONE

Chapter 1 - Of the Girding of a Monk.

In outlining customs and rules for a monastery, where better to begin, under God's guidance, than with the actual monks' habit? Once we have described what we can observe of their exterior appearance, we can better turn to a proper description of their interior attitude. [*Migne's Chapter 2*] Now it is fitting for a monk, like a soldier of Christ always armed and ready for war, to have his loins girt. (*Luke 12:35*) The Holy Scriptures show us that those who first laid the foundations of this way of life in the Old Testament, that is to say Elijah and Elisha, were thus clothed, and in the New Testament also we find the leading men, John the Baptist, Peter and Paul and the others of the same rank, to have been girt in the same way. Elijah, who was the first in the Old Testament to give a splendid example of virginity, chastity and self-control, was sent by the Lord to rebuke the envoys of Ahaziah the sacrilegious king of Israel – for he was suffering from a disease, and had sent to Beelzebub the god of Ekron to enquire over his health. The prophet accosted the envoys and declared that the king would never rise from the bed on which he lay. He was identified for the sick King by the description of his clothing (*II Kg. 1:8*), for when the envoys returned and recounted to him what the Prophet had said, the King asked what sort of man it was who had met them and said these things, and how he was dressed. "A hairy man," they said, "and girt about the loins with a leather belt." From this description the King immediately recognised the man of God, and said "It is Elijah the Tishbite!" It was the belt that indicated him, and the man of God was identified for certain by his hairy and unkempt body, so that among all the thousands of people in Israel he was always marked out by this particular costume as if it were a seal stamped upon him. Of John the Baptist too, who stood like a holy frontier post between the Old Testament and the New, an end and a beginning, we hear in the

Gospel text (*Matth. 3:4*): "This John had a garment made of camel hair, and a leather belt around his loins." Peter too, when he had been thrown into prison by Herod for execution the next day, was commanded by the angel standing by him, "Gird yourself, and put on your sandals." (*Acts 12:8*) God's angel would not have urged him to do this unless he had noticed that he had removed the girdle which normally bound him, so that his tired limbs might rest in sleep. And finally Paul, when he was on his way to Jerusalem where he would soon be thrown into bonds by the Jews, was met in Caesarea by the prophet Agabus. The latter, taking off his loincloth, tied up his hands and feet, performing this action to foreshadow the process of his passion, and saying: "Thus says the Holy Spirit; the man whose belt this is will be bound like this by the Jews in Jerusalem, and given over into the hands of the pagans." (*Acts 21:11*) The prophet could hardly have been able to say "the man whose belt this is", unless Paul were continually accustomed to wear it around his loins.

Chapter 2 - Of a Monk's Tunic.

A monk should also have a tunic which just covers his body, to avoid the embarrassment of nudity, and preserve him from harmful cold; it should not give rise to display or vanity, as the Apostle warns us: "If we have food and clothing, we should be content with that." (*I Tim. 6:8*) "Clothing", he says not "raiment" as some modern translations inaccurately give it, that is to say something which covers the body, not something to preen oneself about. It should be of a common pattern, so that men should not be distinguished from others of their profession by originality in colour or cut; it should not be elaborately adorned, nor easily spoilt by any chance stain. In short, the monks should be distinguished from seculars by their clothing, in such a way that the appearance of the servants of God may preserve a common style for all. For in God's household, anything done by only one person, or by a few, and not generally or throughout the whole community, would be unnecessary or excessive, and should be reckoned dangerous, displaying vanity rather than virtue. That is why unless we can be sure that a tradition derives from the ancient saints who laid the foundations of this way of life, or from the Fathers of our own time who still preserve the customs they inherited from them, it would be best to avoid it as something futile and worthless.

For that reason a shirt of coarse hair, worn in an ostentatious manner for all to see, cannot bring any spiritual benefit, and in fact is a cause of pride; moreover it is a positive hindrance to the carrying out of necessary work (which a monk should always be ready and willing to do) and should never be allowed. Even if we do hear of some worthy men who wore hairshirts, it should not therefore be countenanced by us in a monastic rule, nor should the ancient decisions of the Fathers be set aside just because a few men, relying on the privilege of special virtues, can perform things which are different from the general custom without being blamed for it. For the common universal custom should not be set aside or condemned because of the opinion of a few. Our unwavering trust should be placed in, and our unhesitating obedience should always be given to, those customs and rules which derive from antiquity and the majority of the holy Fathers, handed on in an undisputed tradition, not those introduced by the whim of a minority. Nor may we justify a daily routine on the example either of the sinful King Jehoram of Israel who when surrounded by hordes of enemies tore his tunic and was seen to have a hairshirt on underneath (*II Kg. 6:30*), or of the Ninivites who dressed in harsh hairshirts to ward off the judgement of God pronounced against them by the prophet (*Jonah 3:5*), for the former is proved to have kept such clothing hidden and covered, in that no one would have noticed it had he not torn his tunic; and the latter wore hairshirts publicly at a time when all were bewailing the imminent destruction of their city, all were dressed alike, so that no one could be accused of ostentation. A distinction is only offensive to the common good if it is ostentatious.

Chapter 3 - Of the Egyptian Hood.
Some elements of the habit of Egyptian monks are not intended so

much for physical necessity as for discipline of life, since care for simple innocence can be indicated in the very style of clothing. For they wear tight-fitting hoods which cover the neck and shoulders and conceal the head at all times, both day and night, in order that they may be inspired to imitate the innocence and simplicity of small children even by imitating their costume. Returning to the infancy of Christ, they sing at all hours in loving affection, "O Lord, my heart is not proud, nor are my eyes lifted up, I have not walked among the great, nor among those too wondrous for me. Have I failed to think lowly thoughts, or been arrogant in soul? I am like a suckling on his mother's knee." (*Psalm 130/1*)

Chapter 4 - Of the Egyptian Scapular.
They wear linen scapulars, which only just reach to the elbow and leave the hands uncovered, so that these curtailed garments may suggest that they curtail their worldly concerns and works, and the linen fabric teach them to be restrained from all earthly preoccupations. Thus they can be attentive to the Apostle, saying to them every day: "Mortify your limbs which are upon the earth." (*Col. 3:5*) The same garment cries out to them "You are dead, and your life is hidden in Christ." (*Col. 3:3*) And again: "Now I live, not for myself, but Christ lives in me. For to me the world is crucified, and I to the world." (*Gal 6:14*)

Chapter 5 - Of the Almuce
They also wear a double cape, lined with wool, called an *analobe* in Greek, which we might call a scarf or neckerchief or, to be precise, an almuce. It covers the back of the neck and spreads over the shoulders, its two ends folded over and tied around, so that it gathers in the fullness of the clothing and binds it close to the body. Thus the sleeves are held tight and the arms free and ready for any sort of work, as they try to fulfil the Apostle's command perfectly: "These hands have toiled not only for myself but also for my companions; we have never eaten anyone's bread for nothing, but the fruit of our own work and effort, night and day, lest we be a burden on any of you." (*Acts 22:34*)

And again "If anyone refuses to work, he should not eat." (*II Thess. 3:10*)

Chapter 6 - Of the Cappa.

After this, they cover their neck and shoulders with a light mantle, which in many languages is called a cappa, aiming at economy both in simplicity of dress and cheapness of price, and thus save themselves both the price and the ostentation of a cloak or coat.

Chapter 7 - Of the Fleece or Goatskin.

The last item of the habit is a goatskin, which may be called a fleece or hide, and a staff which they carry in imitation of those who began this way of life in the Old Testament; the Apostle says of them, "They went about in fleeces and goatskins, hungry, poor and distressed, and the world was unworthy of them, wandering through deserts, mountains and caves and hollows in the ground." (*Heb. 11:38*) This costume of goatskin indicates that they should mortify all the urges of the flesh and its emotions, and so remain in earnest pursuit of virtue; and that no trace of the callow headstrongness of youth or their former inconsistency should remain in their bodies.

Chapter 8 - Of the Egyptian Staff.

That these men should carry a staff is taught by Elisha, who was one of them, when he said to his boy Giezi on sending him to raise the woman's son, "Take my staff and run, place it on the boy's face, and he will live." (*II Kg. 4:29*) The prophet would surely have not suggested that action unless it were something he was always accustomed to carry. The spiritual significance of carrying a staff is that the monks should not go unarmed among so many barking dogs of vice, and invisible beasts of spiritual wickedness – the holy David prays to be freed from these, "Do not yield my life, O Lord, into the power of the beasts." (*Psalm 73/4:19*) With the sign of the cross they drive them back and expel them afar, and through being severe with themselves, ever mindful of the Lord's passion, they vanquish them as they imitate what He endured.

Chapter 9 - Of their Footwear.

They avoid wearing shoes, according to the Gospel's recommendation, but since something is demanded by bodily frailty, in the cold of early winter morning or the heat of summer noon, they protect their feet with sandals. They justify this practice as if they had the Lord's permission for it, for while we live in this world we cannot entirely ignore the concerns and discomforts of the flesh, nor be so strong that we are totally unconcerned about them. We must attend to the necessities of the body, but without much care and only slight attachment. The feet of the soul should always be ready, apt for the spiritual race and to proclaim the message of peace, for we run after the "savour of the ointment" of Christ (*Song. 1:2*), and as David says "I ran with desire." (*Psalm 61/2:5*) Jeremiah also says, "I have not toiled in following you ;" (*Jer. 17:16*) it is a grief to us if we are caught up in the death-delivering worries of this world, and are obsessed with matters which are of no use to supply the necessities of nature but lead only to useless and dangerous decadence. We shall avoid this if we refrain from "fixing our sights on pleasure", as the Apostle says. (*Rom. 13:13*) Moreover, although it is permissible to use sandals, as the Lord has conceded, they never allow their feet to be encumbered with them when they approach the altar to celebrate or to receive the Sacred Mysteries, for they consider they should follow literally what was said to Moses and to Joshua son of Nun, "Take the shoes off your feet, for the place where you stand is holy ground." (*Exod. 3:5, Josh. 5:16*)

Chapter 10 - On the Attention which should be paid to the Location, according to the Climate and Local Custom. (Omitted by Migne)

I have included all this so as not to leave out any part of the Egyptian habit. Nevertheless we need only retain those things which our location and custom admit. For our cold winters would not allow us to make do with sandals, scapulars or a single tunic, whereas wearing a tight hood or a sheepskin would only make onlookers laugh without impressing them. Therefore I think we should select out of the garments I have described things which are suitable for the profession of poverty in our climate. Our clothing in general should be respectable and simple, not so ostentatious as to cause scandal among the men of this world.

Chapter 11 - On the Spiritual Girdle and its meaning. (Omitted by Migne)
Once the soldier of Christ has been dressed in these garments, let him first recognise that his girdle constrains him in order to fortify him to be ever ready and willing for all the offices and works of the monastery, not only in mind but in his clothing as well. He will seem all the more eager for spiritual progress and the acquisition of divine knowledge in purity of heart, the more dedicated he be to obedient work. Secondly he should know that the symbolism of being girt with a loincloth is not insignificant. Girding his loins and being wrapt in leather, which is dead skin, signifies that he carries always about with him the mortification of those fleshly members in which the seed of lust is retained, following the gospel command "be your loins girt", (*Luke 12:35*) and always adding St Paul's comment "mortify your members which are on the earth, fornication, uncleanness, lust, evil desires." (*Col 3:5*) We find in Holy Scripture that those who are girt with a girdle are those in whom the seed of generation is extinct, who can repeat the words of the prophet David both in deed and strength, "I am become like a bottle in the frost." (*Ps. 118/9:83*) By the power of the spirit they stretch the dead skin of the outer man, having eradicated the vices of the flesh. He adds "in the frost" meaning that they are not just content with mortifying the heart, but have also congealed with the frost of external continence the motions of the flesh and the impulses of nature itself. They do not carry about within them the reign of sin in their mortal bodies, (as St Paul says, *II Cor. 4:10*), nor do they let their flesh rebel against the spirit.

BOOK TWO

Of the Rule for Night Office
and how to Sing the Psalms

Chapter 1
Once the Soldier of Christ has girded himself with this double armour, he should learn the pattern of regular prayer and psalmody which the holy fathers of the East established. The value of this prayer, and how it is possible to "pray without ceasing" as the Apostle commands, (*I Thess. 5:17*) is something we shall explain, in so far as the Lord allows, when we begin to record the conversations of the elders.

Chapter 2 - Of the varying number of psalms customary in different regions
On this subject, we have come across many in various regions who have invented themselves different structures and rules, as the whim takes them, since they are "zealous for God, but without discretion" as the Apostle says. (*Rom. 10:2*) For some consider that every night they should say twenty or thirty psalms, each of them elaborated with sung antiphons and with some harmonisation; others have even tried to exceed this number, others again say only eight or ten psalms. In this way we have observed different structures in different places, and in fact found as many different forms of the Office in use as the number of monasteries and cells we have visited. When it comes to the day hours of the Office, that is Terce, Sext and None, some have decided to give praise to the Lord appropriately for each hour by making the number of psalms and prayers equal to the number of the hour, while others prefer to allocate six psalms to each office of the day. That is why I think it necessary to set out the most ancient customs of the fathers, as is still practised throughout Egypt among the servants of God, so that the infancy of our newborn monastery may be nourished by the most ancient institutions of the First Fathers.

Chapter 3 - Of the uniform rule kept throughout Egypt, and of the election of superiors over the brothers.

The monasteries of Egypt and the Thebaid are not governed on the whim of any individual recluse, but continue still today according to the old succession and tradition, in which also new foundations are made. Here we can observe the correct rite of the Office both in the evening assembly and in night vigils.

No one is permitted to take the lead over a community of brothers, or even over himself, before he is proved to be superior to all his passions, and aware that he has no rights or authority even over himself. A man who has renounced the world must expect a long probation in the common life, whatever abilities or possessions he might have had, until he be free from any conceit about what he either left behind or brought with him to the monastery. He should be so obedient that "making a new start" in the Lord's words (*Matth. 18:3*) he should renew his lost innocence, taking no account of his age, or the number of years he must consider wasted, squandered in secular life. He must be unhesitatingly obedient even to those younger than himself, recognising the value of the basic training of a fresh recruit to the service of Christ's army. He is trained to accustom himself to manual work, so that he can prepare the daily fare both for his own needs and for any visitors. Thus through the discipline of work he becomes able to forget both the burdens and the comforts of his previous life, and acquire a humble spirit.

For this reason, no one is chosen to direct a community of brothers or destined to be a superior until he has learnt through obedience what he will have to order his subjects, and become accustomed to the customs of the elders which he must pass on to the younger. They declare that it takes a wise man to rule well and to be well ruled; and they define that as the greatest gift of grace from the Holy Spirit. For no one can command those under him in matters that lead to salvation unless he be first trained in all the discipline of virtue; nor can anyone obey an elder unless it be one who is already perfected in the fear of God and the virtue of humility. That is why we discovered varying rites and rules in use in different regions, since we heard that men untrained in the ways of the elders had been placed in charge of monasteries; they made themselves abbots before they were novices, ruling as the whim takes them, more ready to demand observance of their own decisions than to preserve the well-tested teaching of those before them.

We were trying to describe the best possible pattern to be observed in prayer, inspired by the institutes of the Fathers, but we have introduced a matter which we had intended to discuss in its proper place. Now, therefore, let us return to the point.

Chapter 4 - How in Egypt and the Thebaid a total of twelve psalms is customary.
As we were saying, all through Egypt and the Thebaid a total of twelve psalms is customary both at vespers and in the night vigils. After this follow two readings, one from the Old Testament and one from the New. This is the ancient rite, and it has remained unchallenged until today for so many centuries in all the monasteries of that province, because it is believed not to be a human invention appointed by the elders, but to have been revealed to those fathers on the authority of an angel from heaven.

Chapter 5 - Of how an angel revealed the number of twelve psalms.
In the early days of the faith monks were few indeed, but very select. They adopted their way of life from the holy evangelist Mark, of happy memory, who was the first patriarch of the city of Alexandria. To begin with they preserved the splendid tradition of which we read in the Acts of the Apostles, the way of life of the early Church and the crowd of believers: "Of the multitude of believers there was but one heart and one soul; none of them would claim that any of their property was his own, but everything was common to all; those who were owners of lands or houses would sell them and bring the proceeds of the sale to place at the feet of the Apostles; and it was divided up among each as needs arose." (*Acts 4:32-37*) But indeed they improved on this example greatly, for they withdrew to unfrequented

places outside the city and led a life so austere in its privation that their strict discipline of life was the admiration even of those not of our faith. With the same enthusiasm they devoted themselves, by day and by night, to Scripture reading, prayer and manual work, so that their fasting was not interrupted by the desire or even the memory of eating, except every second or third day, when physical hunger compelled them to take food and drink out of necessity, not appetite, and that not before sundown, so that they associated the daylight with concentration on spiritual matters, and the needs of the body with the night. They achieved even more amazing things than this, of which you may read in the Ecclesiastical History, even if you have heard nothing at first hand from those who have lived that life.

So it was at that time that the Church was established in its first perfection, which endured unchanged in successive generations even until living memory, when the fervent faith of the few had not yet cooled by being diffused among a multitude. The worthy fathers took careful consideration, mindful of future generations, to lay down what the rite of daily prayer for all monks should be. They agreed together to pass on an inheritance of peaceful devotion to their successors, safeguarded from all divisive uncertainty, for they were concerned lest disagreement arise about the daily celebration among men living the common life, or lest new variations sow the seeds of future error, jealousy or division. For once it happened that each individual, without thinking of the weakness of others, made decisions based on his own fervour about the method of prayer he thought ideal for his own faith and ability. He would take no account of what might be possible for the majority of the brothers in general, among whom inevitably a large proportion would be weak; this led to competition, each one attempting to decree an absurd number of psalms as his own strength of mind dictated. Some would opt for fifty psalms, some sixty, others would even think themselves bound to surpass that number, and instead of a religious rule they ended up with a pious competition of holy varieties, until the time for the sacred celebration of vespers would be taken up in argument. And then it happened that, among those who wished to celebrate the daily Office, someone stood up in the middle to sing psalms to the Lord. All the others sat (as is still the custom in Egypt), and directed their attention to the words of the psalmist. He sang eleven psalms, on an even tone, with no pause between verses, but separated by collects. The twelfth psalm he sang with an Alleluia response, and then suddenly vanished from the eyes of all, bringing the celebration, and also the debate, to an end.

Chapter 6 - Of the custom of twelve collects.
The council of those worthy fathers understood from this that an angel had acted, on the Lord's behalf, to lay down a general rule for communities of monks, and so decreed that this number of collects should be observed both at vespers and at night vigils. To this they added two readings, from the Old Testament and the New, on their own authority and as it were specially for those who wished and who were assiduous in the study and contemplation of sacred Scripture. On Saturdays and Sundays they took both readings from the New Testament, that is one from the Epistles or the Acts of the Apostles, and the other from the Gospel. Those who were responsible for reading or studying the Scriptures did this every day during Eastertide.

Chapter 7 - Of discipline in Prayer.
These said collects they begin and end in this manner: when the psalm is finished they do not immediately fall to their knees, as some of us do in these parts, where before the psalm is properly over we hurriedly kneel to pray, rushing to finish our devotions as quickly as possible. We seem eager to improve on the rite established for us by antiquity, and cut short the remaining psalms, speeding to the conclusion, more concerned for resting our weary bodies than seeking an ideal form of useful prayer. In Egypt it is not so - but before they kneel down they reflect a while, and pass a longer period standing in prayer. After that they prostrate themselves for a moment, to worship God in his mercy, and rise up very quickly. Standing again they lift their hands as before, and pray upright, pausing wrapt in their own prayer. For they say that

if they lay on the ground for any longer it would be more conducive to sleep than meditation. We have observed this, unfortunately, to be true from our own daily experience. Often enough we have found ourselves wishing to prolong this prostration of the body, not for the sake of prayer but of rest! When he who is to collect up the prayers rises from the ground, all stand with him, and so no one kneels before he does so, nor presumes to remain prostrate after he has stood up, lest he be thought to make his own private prayer rather than follow the intention of the one who makes the collect.

Chapter 8 - Of the prayer that follows the psalm.

The custom observed in our country is that one person sings the conclusion of the psalm, and all stand to sing together "Glory be to the Father and to the Son and to the Holy Spirit", but this is quite unknown in the East, where after the psalm all are silent while the cantor sings the prayer. They are accustomed to use the invocation of the Holy Trinity only to conclude the psalmody.

Chapter 9 - Of the nature of the prayers.

The course of our disquisition on the rites has brought us to the question of how these canonical prayers are made, although we shall find an occasion for a fuller discourse in the Collations of the Elders. There we shall treat of prayer at length, for we have already begun to compose a passage about method and fervour. Nevertheless, I think it is necessary at this stage of our account, where it seems logical, to say a little here about the subject, so that while we are talking about the posture of the exterior man, laying as it were the foundations of prayer, we should take a little trouble to expound the interior state of man, and outline the main points of prayer. At any rate this would ensure that if sudden death were to prevent us from completing the book which, with God's help, we intend to write, we might at least leave you the rudiments of this so necessary subject in the present volume, delaying the full account although you are eager for it. In this way, although we can take a respite from this task, we can at least indicate to you some elements of the art of prayer. This will be of some benefit, especially for those who live in monasteries. At the same time I can take account of those who may chance to come across this little book, and will not be able to find the other, and will learn here instruction in the method of prayer to some extent, so they will not be totally ignorant of how they ought to offer the spiritual sacrifice, now that they are informed about costume and outward bearing. But in fact the present book, which I am hammering out with God's help, is concerned more with the exterior disposition of a man and the institution of a monastery, while the other book will deal more with interior discipline, the perfection of the heart, and the life and teachings of the hermits.

Chapter 10 - How prayer among the Egyptians is made in silence, and briefly.
When they come together to celebrate the above mentioned Offices (which they call *synaxeis*) they keep such a strict silence that although such a huge number of brothers are assembled, you might think there was no one there other than the one in the middle standing and singing the psalm. Especially when the prayer is being made, no one spits, nor hawks, no cough is heard, no sleepy sigh of indrawn or outward breath, neither groan nor murmur are emitted to disturb the standing monks, and no voice is heard save that of the priest who concludes the prayer; unless by chance an ecstasy has forced a sound from the lips, and the heart is taken unaware by the burning fervour of an irresistible and overwhelming spirit, the inflamed mind unable to contain within itself what strives to escape the imprisoning breast in groans too deep for words. Anyone who is so careless as to pray out loud, or produces from his throat any of the sounds I have described, or above all sets everyone yawning, is considered to have sinned in two ways : firstly he is at fault in his prayer, in that he has offered it to God carelessly, and secondly through his uncontrolled outburst he has interrupted the concentration of someone who might perhaps have been able to pray with greater attention. For this reason they bring their prayer to a speedy conclusion, lest, if we stayed long

at it, superfluous spittle or phlegm might disturb the fervour of our prayer. Therefore, while it is still ardent, the prayer must be snatched as if from the jaws of the enemy. He is certainly always on the assault against us, especially when he sees us trying to oppose him through prayer to the Lord. He is quick to draw the mind away from attention to prayer, through distractions, or the rising of various humours, striving by these means to cool us from our first ardour. Therefore they consider that it is more effective to make short prayers, but frequent ones. Frequent, because the more often we entreat the Lord the more closely we can cleave to Him; short, because thus we can frustrate the efforts of the devil who besieges us particularly while we pray.

Chapter 11 - The Egyptian manner of singing psalms.

Now they do not perform the actual psalms which are sung in the assembly by singing them straight through: rather they divide them up with two or three intervals, depending on the number of verses, and make a prayer in between, going through them carefully and clearly. They delight more in understanding the text than in sheer volume. They follow the phrase, "I will sing in the spirit, but I will also sing with my mind", *(I Cor.14:15)* with all their might. They therefore consider it more profitable to sing ten verses with an attentive mind than to pour out the whole psalm in confusion. This confusion often arises through rushing the recitation, when the cantor sees the modes and quantity of psalms still to be sung, and is more concerned to hurry to the end of the office than to open the meaning to his hearers. So if any of the young ones begins to speed up the psalmody too much, either through enthusiasm or through still being inexperienced, the singing is stopped by an older monk, who claps his hand on his seat, and makes everyone stand up to pray. They are always careful that those sitting down are not wearied by too much psalmody, so that the cantor does not only lose the benefit of understanding it himself, but also disadvantages the others, in boring them with the Office by his own excess. They are also always careful to observe that no psalm is said with the Alleluia response unless it is one which is preceded by a title containing "Alleluia." And so they divide up the aforesaid number of twelve psalms so that if there are two brothers they sing six each, if three, four each, if four, three each. They never sing less than that number in their assembly, and no matter how large the congregation, there are never more than four brothers who sing at the Office.

Chapter 12 - Why one sings while the others sit, and how they extend the vigil until dawn in their own cells after the Office.

During the canonical number of twelve psalms which I have described they attend with such bodily stillness that when they celebrate the Office properly in this manner all, except the one who has stood up in the middle to sing, sit on low seats and are totally intent on the voice of the singer with all their hearts. Indeed, they need to be relieved by this concession, for they would be unable to endure standing for even this number of psalms, so wearied are they by fasting and work all day and all night long. For they do not permit any time to pass without some occupation, and they try to work with their hands not only every moment which the day illuminates, but they are also anxious to discover types of work which are not impeded by the very darkest hours of night. They believe themselves the more able to acquire the purest heights of spiritual contemplation the more devoted they are to apply themselves to manual work. That is why they consider that the moderate number of prayers was of divine institution, so that space might be available for their hard work, and they might not be so tired and physically weakened that they conceive any dislike for long prayers. When they have duly finished the canonical offices, each one returns to his own cell. They occupy these either alone, or with at most one companion, their fellow in work, in self-control and the thirst for discipline, or at any rate someone congenial and similar in virtue. There they again carefully celebrate the prayers of the Office as if offering their own sacrifice, and none of them ever returns to sleep, until the dawn breaks and daytime work takes the place of the night's prayer and labour.

Chapter 13 - Why it is not fitting to sleep after the Night Office.

They are careful to keep up this work for two reasons, apart from the fact they consider themselves bound to offer sacrifice to God in the work of their own hands, dependent on their whole-hearted effort. It would be useful for us too to take the same trouble if we are eager for perfection. Firstly, lest the jealous fiend through some dream defile the purity which was gained in the psalms and prayers of the night, angered by our chastity to which he is ever most opposed. Once we have obtained pardon for our ignorant transgressions, and forgiveness begged with tears in confession, he is determined to corrupt us if he finds a moment's chance, and is most anxious to weaken or destroy our confidence when he sees us devoutly turning to God in purity of prayer. Thus he attempts during the short space of this hour after vigils to bring down those whom he failed to defeat all night long. Secondly, lest even if no such dreadful illusion of the devil overwhelm us, blameless sleep burden with sluggish torpor the monk who has to wake so soon, dissipate his energy all through the day, dull the acuteness of his understanding, and exhaust the greatness of heart which could have preserved him all day watchful and strong against the wiles of the foe. That is why the canonical Office is followed by these private prayers in the cell which give them a greater intensity, and so the purity acquired through psalms and prayers is not lost, and the watchful care we preserve during the day is enhanced by the night's meditation.

Chapter 14 - How they apply themselves to manual labour and prayer at once in their cells.

They apply themselves to manual labour to avoid slumber creeping up on the unwary. Just as there is no time allowed by them for idleness, so there is no end allotted to spiritual meditation. For they exercise the powers of body and soul at once, and their inner devotion is equal to their external activity. They use the weight of toil like a fixed and unmoveable anchor to restrain their fleeting emotions and fickle fantastic thoughts, so that within the enclosure of their cell they might confine the busy wandering mind as if in a secure harbour. Thus fixed only on spiritual matters and careful to keep guard over their thoughts, they preserve the mind from corruption not only by not giving in to indecent imaginations, but even by guarding it from unnecessary and neutral thoughts. Hence it is difficult to know which came first, whether they keep at their ceaseless manual work for the sake of spiritual meditation, or whether they acquire this notable light of wisdom and spiritual advancement for the sake of efficient work.

Chapter 15 - How this rule, by which they all return to their cells after the end of Office, preserves modesty, and what blame attaches to those who do otherwise.

So, as we have already said, once they have finished the psalms in their daily assembly, none of them remains even for a moment or dares to chatter with another, and they do not presume to leave their cells for the rest of the day, nor to leave off the work which they do in them, unless they are called out to perform some necessary duty. If they go out for this purpose, they never delay for any conversation. Each one does the task laid on him, such as memorising a psalm or some passage of scripture, and they allow no time for idle chatter, let alone grumbling together or indecent talk, for both lips and heart are continually occupied in spiritual meditation. They take very great care lest any of them spend even the briefest time alone with another monk, particularly a younger one, and they are scrupulous never to go into a private place together nor hold each others' hands. If any of them are discovered to have broken this rule, or been found out in any of the forbidden things, they are considered guilty of no light fault, but to be disobedient, undermining the rule, and not beyond suspicion of party spirit or indecency. No one thus guilty is permitted to attend Office with the monks again until he has purged his guilt by public penance before all the assembled brothers.

Chapter 16 - That no one may pray with one who has been excluded from public prayer.

If anyone is excluded from the public prayer for some sin which he has confessed, no one is permitted to pray with him before he has done penance on his knees, and the abbot has publicly proclaimed his pardon and forgiveness before all the brothers. Because of this rule, they keep themselves apart from associating with his prayer and avoid him, since they consider one who is excluded from public prayer to be "handed over to Satan" as the Apostle decreed. (*I Cor. 5:5*) If anyone is so rash, through inconsidered affection, as to join in prayer with such a one before he has been received back by the superior, he makes himself an associate in his sentence, that is to say voluntarily handing himself over to Satan, to whom the other had been committed for the correction of his fault. In so doing he incurs a greater fault, since in associating with him in common conversation or prayer, he causes the poison of his disobedience to increase, and the sinner's guilt to become greater. For in giving him a comfort which is pernicious, he makes his heart harder and harder, and does not allow him to become humble (which was the purpose of excluding him) so that he takes little account of the superior's rebuke, or considers making a feigned penance and reconciliation.

Chapter 17-That he who wakes the brethren to pray should call them at a regular time. The one who is entrusted with calling the monastic community and announcing the time for the Office, does not presume to waken the brethren for the daily vigils at random, as he chooses, nor whenever he wakes in the night or his own pattern of sleep or wakefulness suggest. Even though the daily routine may cause him to wake at a regular time, nevertheless he should carefully and frequently check the fixed time for the Office by the movement of the stars, and call them to the Office to pray, lest he be found neglectful either by oversleeping and so being late for the proper time of night, or by anticipating the time through fear of falling asleep too soon, so that he might be thought more interested in his own needs of sleep than in helping others to pray or rest.

Chapter 18 - That they do not kneel from Saturday evening to Sunday evening, nor throughout Eastertide.

We should also note that in Egypt, from the evening of Saturday, which will dawn on the Lord's Day, (*Matth. 28:1*) until the following evening they do not kneel, nor do they throughout the days of Eastertide, nor do they then keep the normal fasts. The reason for this will be found in its proper place, when the Lord wills, in the Collations of the Elders. My intention here is to run through these matters briefly, not to exceed the size of book I was asked for, or burden the reader with tedious detail.

BOOK THREE

Of the Rule for Day Office
and how to Sing the Psalms

Chapter 1 - Of Terce, Sext and None, as they are celebrated in Syria.
I think I have said enough, to the best of my abilities and with God's help, about the night Office and how they sing the psalms in Egypt. Now I must treat of the Offices of Terce, Sext and None, according to the rite of the monasteries of Palestine and Mesopotamia; for I promised in the prologue I would by their customs moderate the perfect and impossibly strict discipline of the Egyptians.

Chapter 2 - How in Egypt they apply themselves to prayers and psalms (with accompanying work) throughout the day without distinguishing the time.
The Divine Offices which I am about to describe are kept at set times with intervals between them, and a warning bell; but among the Egyptians they are celebrated on their own, with accompanying work, all day long. For there they apply themselves to manual labour ceaselessly in their private cells, in such a way that they never stop pondering over the psalms or other Scriptures. They intersperse prayers and intercessions from time to time and fill up the course of the day with those Offices which we celebrate at set times. They have no public celebration during the day apart from Vespers and Night Vigils, except on Saturdays and Sundays, when they come together at the third hour of the day to celebrate Holy Mass. That which is offered without intermission is of more value than what is interrupted by intervals, and a spontaneous gift is more pleasing than functions which are ordered by a rule: therefore David rejoices more than usual when he says "I will offer a voluntary sacrifice", (*Psalm 53/4:8*) and "the free offerings of my lips are pleasing to you, O Lord." (*Psalm 118/9:108*)

Chapter 3 - How throughout the East the Offices of Terce, Sext and None are composed of three psalms and prayers, and why these sacred offices are specifically allotted to these times.

Now in the monasteries of Palestine, Mesopotamia and all the East, the offices of the above mentioned hours are composed of three psalms every day. Thus they make constant offering to God at set times, and nothing is able to prevent them fulfilling their spiritual duties in due proportion, and performing the appropriate worship. We hear of the prophet Daniel offering prayers to the Lord by the open window of his chamber at these three hours. (*Dan. 6:13*) Nor is it at random that these hours are particularly appointed for divine worship, for in them was achieved the fulfilment of the promise and the consummation of our redemption.

At the third hour the Holy Spirit which the prophets had foretold is first seen descending upon the Apostles as they meet for divine worship. For when the unbelieving crowd of Judaeans were amazed at the fluency of speech which had come upon them through the inpouring of the Holy Spirit, and mockingly said they must be full of new wine, Peter stood up before them and said: "Men of Israel, and all you inhabitants of Jerusalem, let me inform you, listen to my words. These men are not drunk as you believe, for it is but the third hour, but this is what was spoken of by the prophet Joel, 'And it will come to pass in the latter days, says the Lord, that I will pour out my Spirit upon all flesh; your sons and your daughters shall prophesy, your young men shall see visions, and your old men shall dream dreams. And indeed I shall pour out my Spirit in those days upon my servants and upon my handmaids, and they shall prophesy.'" (*Acts 2:14-18*) These things, we can see, were done at the third hour, and the coming of the Holy Spirit foretold by the prophets was fulfilled upon the Apostles at that time.

At the sixth hour our Lord and Saviour was offered to the Father as a perfect victim, and ascended the Cross for the salvation of all the world; he absolved the sins of the human race, "despoiled the principalities and powers", (*Col. 2:15*) openly overthrew them, and liberated us all who were suffering and bound under the unbearable burden of an accusation which he snatched up from court and nailed to the trophy of his Cross. At the same hour, while Peter was wrapt in prayer, there was revealed to him the calling of the Nations, as the vessel of the Gospel was let down from heaven, and all kinds of animals which were contained in it were made clean, as a voice from heaven spoke to him, "Arise, Peter, kill and eat." (*Acts 10:13*) The vessel which was let down from heaven by four handles is clearly understood to symbolise the Gospels, for although there seem to be four distinct beginnings of the fourfold Gospel narrative, yet there is only one body of the Gospel, which is comprised of the birth and divinity of Christ, his miracles and passion. It is well said that the vessel was "like linen", not "of linen", for linen is a badge of penance, and since the death of the Lord took place not through the laws of human nature but at His own will, it is called "like" linen. For though he died according to the flesh, he did not die according to the spirit, since "his soul was not abandoned into Hell, nor did his flesh see corruption." (*Psalm 15/16:10*) And again he says "No one takes my life from me, but I lay it down of my own free will. For I have the power to lay it down, and I have the power to take it up again." (*John 10:18*) So through this vessel of the Gospels, which was decreed by heaven and written by the Holy Spirit, all the nations which were once placed outside the keeping of the law, and therefore counted unclean, are now brought together in the obedience of faith. They have been saved and cut away from the cult of idols, to proceed to the saving banquet, and declared pure at the authoritative voice of Peter.

At the ninth hour the Lord burst into Hell and in the splendour of his countenance dispersed the deep infernal darkness, shattered the bronze doors and broke the bars of iron. He took captive the captivity of the saints who were held imprisoned in the fearful darkness of Hell, saved them and brought them with him to heaven; he withdrew the fiery sword and restored to paradise its first inhabitant who acknowledged him with love. It was at the same hour that the centurion Cornelius applied himself to prayer with his usual piety, and an angel spoke to him to say that his prayers and good deeds had been presented before the Lord, and again at the ninth hour the sacraments were opened to him, fulfilling the destiny of the nations that had been revealed to Peter in his ecstasy at the sixth hour. (*Acts 10*) And in another place in the Acts of the Apostle we are told of the same hour, for "Peter and John went up to the temple at the ninth hour of prayer". (*Acts 3:1*)

Here we can clearly see that it was not inappropriate for the Apostles and holy men to dedicate these hours to religious observance; and they should be observed by us in the same way. For unless we had some rule to constrain us to perform this holy service at least at these set times, we would squander the whole of the day wrapt in forgetfulness, or idleness, or business without any interval of prayer. Now what should we say about the evening sacrifice, which even the Old Testament Law of Moses strictly commanded should be offered? The morning holocausts and evening sacrifices offered daily in the Temple were figurative indeed, but they foreshadow the eternal offering of which David sings, "My prayer is addressed to you like incense in your sight, the raising of my hands like the evening sacrifice". (*Psalm 140/1:2*) This passage is best understood of the true Evening Sacrifice, either because it was instituted on the evening that the Lord dined with his apostles, when he inaugurated the Most Holy Mysteries of the Church, or because on the following day he offered the Evening Sacrifice to the Father, at the very end of the ages, by lifting up his hands for the salvation of the whole world. The extension of his hands upon the Cross may indeed be called a "lifting up", for he lifted up to heaven all of us who were lying in Hell, according to the promise he had made, saying "When I am lifted up from the earth, I will draw all things to me". (*John 12:32*) We find instruction on the morning offering in that it was customary to sing in the morning, "O God my God, I call to you at dawn.... I will ponder on you in the morning", (*Psalm 62/3:2,7*) and again "I awoke early and cried out.... My eyes watched for you at dawn, that I might ponder your word". (*Psalm 118/9:147-8*) At these hours also the householder in the Gospel led his labourers into the vineyard. (*Matth. 20:1-16*) He is described as leading them out at the first hour, which is the time set for our morning celebration, and then at the third, sixth and ninth hours, and finally at the eleventh hour at which the hour of the Lamplighting is fixed.

Chapter 4 - How the morning prayer [i.e. Prime] was not established by ancient tradition but was devised in our own time for a particular reason.

It should be recognised that the morning prayer which is now kept especially in western regions was first established as a canonical Hour n my own lifetime in my own monastery, in the place where the Lord Jesus Christ was born of the Virgin and deigned to accept growth as a human infant, and where he strengthened my own feeble infancy in religious life with his grace. For up to that time we find that our predecessors had abandoned the remaining hours to bodily repose once they had completed the daily vigils together with the dawn praise (which in Gallic monasteries is usually celebrated after a little pause once the night psalms and collects are finished). For taking advantage of this laxity they lazily extended the hours of sleep, since they were not compelled to come out of their cells or even rise from their beds for a common celebration until the third hour. The effort of work, and the varied business which they had to attend to during the day, burdened them with excessive fatigue, especially on those days when keeping watch from the evening office up to just before the dawn celebration caused an even greater tiredness.

Certain of the brothers, of a more zealous spirit, were much displeased with this sort of negligence, and brought their complaint to the superiors, who decreed, after long and careful consideration together, that until sunrise when it first becomes possible to read without difficulty, or to take up a manual task, they might let their tired bodies rest, but then, when called after the custom of the monastery, all should rise together from their beds and celebrate three psalms with their collects, in the way in which Terce and Sext were traditionally celebrated. They decided this on the model of the threefold confession of faith, and by this reasonable compromise signalled the end of sleep and the beginning of work.

Now although this office was invented for a particular occasion, and was established in living memory for the reason we have seen, nevertheless it clearly literally fulfils the number which the holy David foretold, (though this is also susceptible of a spiritual interpretation) : "Seven times in the day I have spoken praise to you for the rightness of your judgements". (*Psalm 118/9:162*) For by adding this Office, we make seven meetings for prayer in the course of the day, and are shown to be "speaking praise to the Lord seven times in the day." And so this custom made its way from the East to be usefully observed here, and it has been occasionally observed in some of the most ancient monasteries of the East which never suffer the original rule of the Fathers to be changed.

Chapter 5 - That after Prime it is not fitting to return to sleep.
Some in this province, who were ignorant of why this office was invented and established, go back to bed after singing Prime, taking no account of the problem which the superiors established this office to prevent. For they hurry through saying this office to give time for the lazy and less well intentioned to return to bed. This should in no way happen, as we saw in the previous book in describing the Egyptian office, lest the purity which we gain through humble confession and prayer before dawn be tainted by the rising overflow of natural humours, or corrupted by the deception of the fiend, or simply that our spiritual zeal be weakened by an interval of sleep, however pure and blameless, and we be rendered drowsy and sluggish throughout the day through the after-effects of sleep. To avoid this, the Egyptians (even though they rise before cockcrow at some times of the year) extend the vigils until dawn, after the canonical Office is celebrated, so that the morning light finds them firm in their spiritual zeal, and all day long they are kept alert and eager, ready for the conflict and strengthened against the noonday devil by their nightly exercise in vigils and spiritual meditation.

Chapter 6 - That when the office of Prime is added, the superiors should not alter the original order of the psalms.

We must also be aware that the superiors who decided to add this office of Prime considered nothing should be changed in the ancient order of the psalms, but the Office of night Vigils should be celebrated exactly the same as before. Moreover the psalms of praise [Lauds] which in these parts follow the morning office, they still sing in the same way at the end of night Vigils (which usually comes after cockcrow and before dawn) - these are the hundred and forty eighth psalm which begins "Praise the Lord from the heavens", and the two following. And we know that the fiftieth psalm, the sixty second and the eighty-ninth are appointed for this new little Office. But throughout Italy today at the end of the vigil psalms they sing the fiftieth psalm in all their churches, which I doubt not is a custom that originated there and no where else.

Chapter 7 - That he who does not arrive at the day office before the first psalm is finished may not enter the oratory, but in the night office lateness may be excused to the end of the second psalm.

He who does not arrive at the oratory for Terce, Sext or None before the first psalm is finished should not presume to enter the oratory later nor join in with those who are chanting, but should stand outside and wait for the end of the office, when everyone comes out and he can beg pardon for his carelessness or slowness, penitent and prostrate on the ground. He should know that his laziness cannot otherwise be expiated, but he will not be admitted even to the office that follows three hours later unless he is quick to make satisfaction for his negligence, straightaway and in true humility. However in the night office, pardon is extended to the latecomer up to the end of the second psalm, as long as he hastens to join the community before the brothers kneel in prayer at the end of that psalm. But if he delay even in the slightest beyond the exact time of this concession, he is subject to the same blame and penance which we have already described.

Chapter 8 - The duration, and the order for celebrating the vigils which are kept from the lamplighting on the evening before Saturday.

Every week from the lamplighting on the eve of the Sabbath, Vigils are kept; the superiors allowed that these be celebrated until the fourth cockcrow in winter, when the nights are longer, so that after watching all the night the monks may rest their bodies for the remaining two hours, lest lack of sleep oppress them for the whole of the day. They are as content with this short time of rest as with a whole night's sleep. So we too ought to retain this observance, being content with the sleep granted us from the end of Vigils till dawn, that is until the morning psalmody; we should occupy the whole of the daytime in work and necessary business. We must not be forced by lazy and care-less watching to recover by day the sleep which we stole from the night; we should not think that we have deprived our bodies of rest, but rather that we have turned the time of silence into a nocturnal refreshment. Our weak flesh cannot possibly be totally deprived of rest at night, if we are to be awake and alert in the following day with-out the mind being tired and the soul sluggish. Unless after the end of Vigils it finds a little sleep, the body is hampered, not improved. Therefore one hour of sleep, as we have said, if it is granted before the dawn breaks, will reap the benefit of the hours of watching in which we have passed the whole night. By granting our nature its due, we will not need to make up by day what we have taken from the night. One who tries to deny his physical nature totally, instead of more rea-sonably denying it in part, would have to pay back its due, for he would be, truly, cutting off not what is superfluous but what is necessary. Therefore the profit gained by Vigils would be lost in a greater debt if they were inconsiderately and unreasonably lengthened until the dawn. They are therefore divided into three nocturns so that by separating and varying the work, bodily weariness might be relieved by some diversity. For after they have stood to sing three psalms antiphonally, they sit on the ground or on low stools and respond to three psalms sung by a single cantor, who is appointed one at a time, the brothers taking it in turns. Then, while they still sit in the same silence, three lessons are read. So it happens that they can minimise the bodily effort in order to celebrate Vigils with greater alertness of mind.

Chapter 9 - Why Vigils are prescribed for the eve of the Sabbath, and why throughout the East they relax the fast on the Sabbath.

From the time when the apostles preached, and the Christian faith and religion were established, it has been the rule throughout the East that Vigils should be celebrated on the night before the Sabbath, because our Lord and Saviour was crucified on the sixth day of the week, and the disciples, appalled by the suffering he had just undergone, remained watching all that night, never letting their eyes close in sleep. And so from that time on the Office of Vigils was appointed for that night, and is still observed in the same manner to this day in the whole of the East. Therefore fasting is relaxed on the Sabbath Day, after this wearisome Vigil, as the same apostolic fathers decreed, and this is a lawful custom in all the eastern Churches, according to that verse of Ecclesiastes, which says, "Give a portion to these seven, and indeed to these eight". (*Eccles. 11:2*) This may well have another mystical meaning but can be applied to this case, in that we are urged to give a share in the celebration to the seventh day as well as to the eighth. For the fast is not relaxed for the sake of joining in the Jewish festival, especially among those who can be seen to be quite free of Jewish superstitions, but it is for the recovery of the weary body, as we have said. All through the year they fast for five days of the week, and unless they were refreshed by at least two days remission, they would soon become weak and break down.

Chapter 10 - How it happens that they fast on Saturday in Rome.

Ignorant of the reason for this moderation, there were those in some Western cities, especially in Rome, who thought that this Sabbath relaxation was in no way to be taken, for they say that the Apostle Peter fasted on that day in preparation for his confrontation with Simon Magus. But this is all the more clear evidence that it was not his rule to fast then, but he was compelled to fast by a pressing emergency. For they say Peter asked his disciples for a special fast for that occasion, rather than a normal one, which he would not have done if he had known they used to fast that day as a regular custom. Indeed he would have asked them to do the same even on the Lord's Day if he had been forced to it by the occasion of such a confrontation, and that would not have been immediately fixed as a canonical rule! He did not establish a general custom, but was compelled by necessity to do it once.

Chapter 11 - How the observance of Sunday is kept differently from other days.
We should not fail to notice that on the Lord's Day only one office is celebrated before dinner. They recite their psalms, collects and readings with greater dignity and solemnity out of respect for the assembly of the Lord's Communion, and they count this as fulfilling Terce and Sext together. Thus they do not diminish any of the set prayers, nor of the readings which are annexed, but there is still a difference, or a relaxation as it seems to the brethren, out of respect for the Lord's Resurrection above ordinary days. It seems like a rest from the observance they keep during the week, especially because it is an intermission, marking out that day as a holiday to be awaited reverently, and makes the fasting of the coming week seem less daunting. For a burden is always taken on more easily and work is performed with less effort, if some variety is interspersed, or there succeeds a change of activity.

Chapter 12 - On the days when a dinner is prepared for the brothers, a psalm is not said as they go to eat, unlike when they have lunch.
And so on the days when both a lunch and a dinner are usually offered to the brethren, that is Saturday and Sunday, or on feast days, they do not say a psalm at the evening meal, neither when they arrive at dinner, nor when they rise from it. They still do this for lunch, and for the collation on a canonical fast-day, which is preceded and concluded by fixed psalms. They go to dinner after a short prayer and again when they rise from table they conclude with just a prayer. This is because

this meal is out of the ordinary for monks, and they are not all obliged to take part in it; it is for monks who arrive on a journey, or those who are urged to it by bodily weakness, or at their own discretion.

BOOK FOUR

Of the Training of the Monks

Chapter 1 - On the Training of those who forsake the World, and on how those who enter monasteries in Tabenna or Egypt are treated.

The plan of our treatise now leads us from the canonical order by which the psalms and prayers should be recited in the daily office to speak of the training of one who forsakes this world. First we shall attempt to describe briefly the conditions on which one who aspires to be dedicated to the Lord is received into the monastery, combining some elements from the Egyptian rules and some from those of Tabenna, a monastery in the Thebaïd which has not only greater numbers but also stricter rules than the rest. Indeed more than five thousand brothers live there, governed by one abbot, and obedience is so strong that this huge number of monks is ever subject to its superiors, whereas among us one is scarcely able to command the obedience of another for the very briefest period.

Chapter 2 - How they persevere in the monastery until the extremest old age.

I consider that we should first look at how they persevere for so long, how their humility and obedience last so long, and by what formation they are trained to remain in the monastery until bowed by age. For their life is such as we cannot imagine anyone in our own monasteries enduring for so much as a year, but when we observe how they begin their life of renunciation, we can understand how it comes to pass that they build such an edifice of perfection on such firm foundations.

Chapter 3 - How those who are to be admitted to the monastery are examined.

Now no one who aspires to join the monastery is admitted until he has slept at the gateway for ten days or more, giving proof of his persistence and intentions, as well as his humility and patience. He kneels at the feet of all the brothers as they pass, deliberately rejected and despised by all, as if he were drawn to enter the monastery not out of piety but from need. He is so laden with slights and rebukes that by his patience under stress he may give evidence of his endurance, and how he will cope with temptation. Once his intentions have been thus examined he is received and very carefully searched lest he remain attached to so little as a single coin from his previous wealth. They know full well that no one can persevere in monastic discipline, nor be able to acquire the virtues of humility or obedience, nor be happy in the simplicity and poverty of the community if the slightest amount of money remain concealed in his heart. Indeed as soon as any sort of trouble first arose he would be prompted by reliance on that sum to flee the monastery like a recoiling catapult.

Chapter 4 - Why those who are admitted to the community are not permitted to bring anything with them.
For this reason they do not even accept money from him for the use of the community. Firstly, lest he be proud of his contribution and reluctant to consider himself equal to the poorer brothers; secondly lest this pride prevent him from descending to the lowliness of Christ until he is unable to endure the discipline of the monastery, and leaves it, and then in cooling ardour attempts to reclaim and demand back what in the first enthusiasm of his spiritual renunciation he had donated, in a sacrilegious spirit which would damage the community. They have learnt from much experience to make this rule for all occasions. For some have been too easily received into other less prudent monasteries, and subsequently attempted to reclaim, with great scandal, the things which they had given and had been consecrated to God's work.

Chapter 5 - Why those who forsake the world, once received into the monastery, put aside their own clothes and are clothed anew by the abbot.
For the same reason, once he is received he is stripped of all his earlier property to the extent that he is not even allowed to keep the very

clothing he wears, but he is brought into the middle of the assembled brethren and undressed of his own garments to be clothed at the abbot's hands with the monastic habit. In this way he comes to know that he has been stripped not merely of all his former possessions, but even of all worldly dignity, to descend to the simple poverty of Christ, and that he will be supported no longer on money acquired by secular skill, nor the proceeds of investments from before he became a Christian, but that he will receive the reward of his service from holy and devout gifts to the monastery. From now on he will be clothed and fed from this source, and have nothing of his own; moreover he will learn to take no care for the morrow, as the Gospel says, *(Matth. 6:34)* nor will he blush at being made equal with the poor, that is the rank of the brethren, among whom Christ is numbered, who was not ashamed to be called their brother; indeed he will be delighted in becoming the equal of his own servants.

Chapter 6 - Why the clothing in which the novice enters the monastery is preserved by the bursar.
The garments which he takes off are assigned to the bursar and preserved until they are well satisfied as to his progress, his way of life and his ability to endure various trials and difficulties. If they perceive that he is able to persevere there for the future, and to remain with the same zeal as when he began, the clothes are distributed to the poor. But if instead they observe in him any habit of grumbling or the fault of even slight disobedience, they strip him of the monastic habit he wears and send him away dressed in the former clothing which had been kept for him. For he has no right to depart with what he had been given, nor do they permit anyone to wear the habit if they have once seen him decline in zeal for the regular life. Thus no one is permitted to depart openly with monastic property : he either escapes in the night like a runaway slave, or is adjudged unworthy of profession in monastic life and is stripped of his habit and expelled in public disgrace before the assembled brethren.

Chapter 7 - Why novices are not immediately permitted to associate with the monks but are first assigned to the guesthouse.

When someone has been received, and shown himself to be persistent, as we have said, he abandons his former clothes and is girt with the monastic habit. He is not immediately allowed to mingle with the community of the brothers, but is assigned to an older monk who lives apart not far from the gate of the monastery, and is in charge of looking after pilgrims and strangers, careful to offer them a charitable welcome. When the novice has worked there for a whole year and demonstrated his care for the pilgrims without any grumbling, if he has acquired humility and patience by this first formation, and is sufficiently tested by this lengthy occupation, he is admitted to associate with the congregation of the brothers. Then he is assigned to another older monk who is responsible for ten juniors, entrusted to him by the abbot, whom he is to train and direct - just as we read in Exodus was done by Moses. (*Exod. 18:25*)

Chapter 8 - By what formation the juniors are first trained to overcome all their passions.

The junior master's chief concern and skill is to teach the junior to overcome his primal urges so that he may succeed in rising even to the summit of perfection. He trains him carefully and rigorously, and constantly takes pains to give him orders which he feels will be contrary to his inclination. They have learnt from long experience that a monk, especially a young one, will never be able to control his lustful passions unless he has first learnt to mortify his inclinations through obedience. Hence they teach that there is no chance of succeeding in eliminating anger, depression or sexual desire, nor of acquiring lowliness of heart, or lifelong affection for the brothers, nor of preserving a real and lasting accord, nor even of remaining very long in the monastery, unless he has first learnt to overcome his inclinations.

Chapter 9 - Why the juniors are instructed to conceal none of their thoughts from their master.

So it is by this formation that they urge their novices to absorb quickly the alphabet and rudiments, as it were, of perfection, and to learn them, so that it may become clear whether they are grounded in real humility or just an outward show of it. To reach this stage easily, they train them never to keep their immodest thoughts hidden through shame in their hearts, but to bring them out immediately and reveal them to the master; nor should they make their own decisions or judgements about them, but believe them to be sinful or not as is decided after discussion with the master. In this way the sly fiend can never outwit the young monk through ignorance or inexperience, nor entangle him in his wiles, since he can see that he is defended not by his own wisdom but by that of his master. Nor can he persuade him to conceal from the master the insinuations which he launches at his heart like burning arrows. The wily serpent can in no way trick or deceive a junior unless he can induce him to draw a veil over his thoughts out of pride or shame. It is therefore considered a general and reliable indication of a thought being from the devil if we are ashamed to reveal it to our superior.

Chapter 10 - How great is the obedience of the juniors even in matters of necessity. As well as this practice, they keep such a rule of obedience that the juniors may not, without the knowledge or permission of their master, so much as leave the room, nor even presume to satisfy the common demands of nature on their own authority. They are so eager to carry out without question whatever he asks them to do, as if they were commanded by God from heaven, that when occasionally impossibilities are asked of them, they obey with such trusting devotion that they try to carry them out wholeheartedly and without the slightest hesitation. Through reverence for their master, they do not baulk at the impossibility of an order. I will not here give particular examples of this obedience, but will set some out in their own place a little further on, if the Lord gives me the opportunity, at your prayers. Now let us look at the remaining aspects of the training, passing over those things which cannot be practicably introduced or carried out in the monasteries of our country, as I promised in the preface that I would do. For instance they do not wear wool but linen, and only one layer, the changing of which is organised by each junior master for his own ten monks when he sees that the ones they are wearing are dirty.

Chapter 11 - What sort of food they consider best.
I shall also pass over the severe and impressive degree of asceticism which brings them to consider the greatest delicacy set before the brothers to be vegetables (which they call *labsanion*) seasoned with salt and steeped in water. There are other such things which in our country neither the climate nor our own weakness could tolerate; I shall only describe things which nothing but a weak will and a sluggish mind could impede, where neither bodily weakness nor geographical location can serve as excuse.

Chapter 12 - How when one knocks on the door they are so eager to run and answer that they leave all work unfinished.
Now when they are seated in their cells, devoting themselves at the same time to work and meditation, and hear the sound of knocking on the door, and the doors of the other cells being knocked (which is the summons to prayer or some other duty), each one immediately emerges from his cell. Thus one who is engaged in writing does not presume to finish a letter which he has been interrupted in beginning, but at the exact moment when the sound of the knocker reaches his ears he leaps up swiftly, and does not delay even so long as to finish the point of a flourish he has begun, but leaves the outlines of the letter unfinished. Eager less for the profit or benefit of the work than for the virtue of obedience, he hastens with wholehearted devotion. They rank obedience not only above manual labour but over reading, silence, the peace of the cell, even before all virtues; they consider all things to take second place to this, and are happy to undergo any inconvenience if only they can show they have in no way infringed this one good thing.

Chapter 13 - How great a disgrace it is for one to claim that even the slightest thing is his own.

I hardly think it necessary among the virtues of their training to notice this further point, that none of them are permitted to have a box or basket of their own, nor to secure anything as private property by a personal mark. We know that they are completely destitute, and have no more than a scapular, mantle, sandals, fleece and a mat. Even in those monasteries where some things are rather lax, this rule can be found most carefully observed even today, so that no one is so bold as even to mention that something is his own, and it is a great disgrace for a monk to utter "my bible", "my notebook", "my pen", "my tunic", "my sandals." In fact they have to make satisfaction by fitting penance if such words chance to slip from their mouths through carelessness or ignorance.

Chapter 14 - How even if one monk's work brings in much money, he must not presume to exceed the simple allowance permitted.

If one of them through his daily work and his own effort brings in a great income for the monastery, enough not only to provide for his own sustenance but even to support the needs of many others, let him be in no way proud of this nor boast of the effort and profit of his work, but never presume to take anything for himself worth more than a couple of buns (which are hardly worth threepence in those parts). Among them no private work is even mentally envisaged, let alone carried out - would that such a custom were as unknown in our own monasteries, I say with shame! When one believes his subsistence to lie entirely in the storeroom of the monastery, he may lay aside all worry and concern, as if he were master of all things in all matters. In order to maintain his determined life of poverty, he strives to preserve it perfect and inviolable for ever; thus he may consider himself cut off from all things and estranged from all, so as to bear himself like a pilgrim, a citizen of the world; rather a child of the monastery, a servant, than master of anything at all.

Chapter 15 - How we are far too concerned with possessions.

What can we poor fools say to this, we who live in monasteries under the structured rule and care of an abbot, but carry around our own keys, to the shame and confusion of our whole profession of life? We are not even ashamed to wear rings publicly on our fingers, wherewith to seal up our private things. Boxes and baskets are not enough, even chests and cupboards do not suffice to hold the property we have amassed, or which we have kept by us when we left the world. And we occasionally get incensed over the slightest trifle, claiming it indeed as our own; if anyone presumes to touch any of this property with a fingertip we are so enraged against him that we cannot restrain our anger from showing itself, not in words alone but in our whole quivering bodies. Let us pass over our own vices, and keep quiet about these things which are beneath our mention, following the psalmist in saying "let my tongue not speak of human affairs"; (*Psalm 16:4*) rather let us continue the account we have begun of the virtues which the Egyptian monks already have, and which we should be striving to attain. We shall describe their rules and briefly give some examples, so that we can move on to certain actions and works of the elders which we have been careful to commit to memory, and in so doing confirm with overwhelming evidence the subjects under consideration. Everything we are saying will be backed up with authoritative examples from their lives.

Chapter 16 - Of the rules about correcting different things.

If anyone accidentally breaks an earthenware mug (which they call a beaker) he can only expiate his crime by public penance; when all the brothers are assembled together he asks pardon lying on the ground while the divine office is being recited, supplicant until the abbot considers it time to bid him stand up. Satisfaction is made in the same way if anyone come late when summoned to work or the customary meetings; or if he giggle slightly while singing a psalm. Likewise if he speak unnecessarily, too harshly or argumentatively, if he be careless in carrying out his responsibilities, if he grumble in the slightest, if he prefer reading to work or obedience, and is therefore sluggish in performing the duties laid on him, if he return not at once to his cell when the office is concluded, if he keep company with another even for a short time, or withdraw somewhere for a moment, if he hold another's hand, or presume to hold conversation with one who is not his room-mate; if he pray with one who is suspended from the oratory, if he try to see any relation or worldly friend or speak to them without his master's presence, if he receive a letter from anyone or try to write one without the abbot's permission. A spiritual rebuke of this nature is sufficient for these and similar things. As for other sins, which are carelessly committed among us, but which we do consider to be blameworthy, such as open quarrelling, public scorn, self-opinionated pride, free and unrestricted visiting, familiarity with women, anger, strife, jealousy and disagreement, taking on private work, the taint of greed, longing for and actually possessing unnecessary things which other brothers do not have, taking extra food secretly, or anything like this - such things are not atoned for by spiritual rebukes but by beating or expulsion.

Chapter 17 - By what authority spiritual books are read in the refectory while the brothers eat, and what a deep silence is kept by the Egyptians.
We know that the custom of reading spiritual books while the brothers eat does not derive from the Egyptians but from the Cappadocians. It was certainly instituted not so much for the sake of spiritual formation, as to restrain idle and unnecessary chatter, and particularly arguments which often arise during meals. They decided to begin this practice, having discovered that they could not prevent arguments among themselves any other way. Among the Egyptians on the contrary, particularly in Tabenna, they keep such a strict silence that when the large number of brothers sit down to take their meal no one presumes even to whisper except the dean who is in charge of each ten monks. When he notices that anything needs to be brought to the table or taken away, he asks for it by signs rather than words. This rule of silence is so well kept among the diners that they draw their hoods

down over their eyes, lest unrestricted sight take the opportunity of wandering too widely, and they see nothing but the table and the food placed on it or which they take up from it, so that none of them notices in what manner or how much any other one eats.

Chapter 18 - How it is forbidden for anyone to take food or drink other than at the common table.

They take very great care that no one is so bold as to take any food or drink into his mouth away from the table and before or after the proper common mealtime. If they go through a garden or orchard where fruit hang temptingly from the trees on all sides, not only brushing against the bodies of the passers-by but even displaying themselves lying on the ground to be trodden underfoot - so easy to pick up and a strong attraction to those who see them, exciting desire, and in their abundance and accessibility enticing men no matter how careful and abstinent they be - but the monks consider it sacrilege not only to taste them but even to touch fruit with their hands, except for those which are publicly laid before them all in the common refectory, and served by the brothers who wait on the others at the bursar's discretion.

Chapter 19 - How the daily duties are carried out by the brothers in Palestine and Mesopotamia.

Not to omit any element of monastic training, I think I must briefly notice how the daily duties are observed by the brothers in other regions. For throughout Mesopotamia, Palestine, Cappadocia and all the East, every week the brothers take turns succeeding each other so that an appropriate number of servers is allotted to the number of monks. They fulfil their duties more carefully and humbly than any slave does for the strictest and most powerful master. Not content merely with the duties laid upon them by the law of the monastery, they even rise in the night to relieve those who have particular duties, and compete in secretly carrying out tasks which others were to have done. Each one takes on duties for a week and performs his office until supper on Sunday. After that the week's service is completed in this manner: when the brothers come together for the psalms which they usually sing before sleep [Compline], those leaving office wash the feet of all, faithfully expecting the reward of a blessing for the work of the whole week. The prayer of the whole brotherhood, following this *mandatum* of Christ, may intercede for any ignorant mistakes or failings committed through human weakness, and commend to God the completed work they have lovingly done, like an acceptable sacrifice. Then on Monday, after morning office, they hand over to their successors the utensils and vessels they had been using. These are so carefully looked after that none of them are lost or damaged, for they know that they will have to give an account for the smallest pots as if they were sacred vessels, not only to the bursar but also to our Lord, if it happen that through their carelessness any of them be damaged. You can see how this discipline works and what faithful care they take, by one example which I shall give you. I am trying to satisfy your eagerness to know as much as possible about everything, and you want me to repeat in this book even things which you know very well - I am just afraid of exceeding a reasonable length!

Chapter 20 - Of the three lentils found by the Bursar.
During a certain brother's week of duty the Bursar happened to be passing and saw three lentils lying on the ground, which had spilled, with the water they were steeped in, from the weekly server's hands while he was hurrying to prepare the meal. The bursar straightaway asked the abbot about this, and the brother was condemned to be suspended from oratory as a spoiler and waster of holy goods. His guilt for this carelessness could not be atoned otherwise than by public penance. For not only do they believe that they themselves do not belong to themselves, but that everything they have is sacred to our Lord, so that if anything is once brought into the monastery, they ought to treat it with great reverence as if it were sacred. They acquire and distribute things so faithfully, even things which seem insignificant, trivial and mean, that if they move them to another place, or arrange them more efficiently, if they fill a beaker with water

51

or give anyone a drink out of it, if they remove so much as a straw from oratory or cell, they confidently trust they will receive from our Lord their just reward.

Chapter 21 - *Of the voluntary extra work some brothers do.*

We have heard of some brothers during whose week there occurred such a shortage of wood that there was not enough to cook the usual meal for the community, so that until more could be acquired and brought, the abbot had decreed that all should be content with dry vegetables and that no one could have any hope of cooked food. The serving brothers, as if cheated of the fruit and reward of their labour through being unable to prepare the usual food for the brethren in their turn, took on a voluntary extra effort and concern. Since they lived in a dry and barren region, where wood cannot possibly be found save by cutting from fruit-trees (not like our own dense woodland), they set off through the wild waste and reached the wilderness which lies near the Dead Sea, to gather in their arms the twigs and thorns which the wind blew hither and thither, and so they prepared the whole meal out of their own unbidden effort. Of the usual repast nothing was missing, as they carried out their duties to the brothers with such diligence. Although the shortage of wood or the abbot's command could have reasonably excused them, they were reluctant to take advantage or lose the reward of their labours.

Chapter 22 - *Of the Egyptian manner of daily duty among the brothers.*

I have described the pattern of service found throughout the East, which, as I said at first, I consider ought to be followed in our own country. However in Egypt, which is the principal subject of my work, they do not have the weekly exchange of service, lest everyone be hindered in the divine office by these duties: responsibility is entrusted to a single chosen brother, a cellarer or cook, who can do the duty well, either for life or for as long as his strength or age permit. He is not burdened by much physical labour, for it does not take great effort to prepare their meals or to cook, since they generally eat dry or raw food, and their greatest delicacies are leek leaves, vegetables rubbed with salt, olives and tiny salt fish (which are called *maenomenia*).

Chapter 23 - Of the Obedience of Abba John, through which he attained even the grace of prophecy.

Since this book is about the training of those who renounce the world, and are thus brought to real humility and perfect obedience, which enables them to rise to the heights of the other virtues, I think I ought to tell you as examples some stories of the elders showing how this virtue excelled in them, as I promised. I shall choose a few specimens from many, so that those who are eager to follow the best path may not only be incited to perfect life but even find a model of how to proceed. I shall tell you just two or three stories from such a countless number of fathers, to make this book worthwhile.

Firstly - Abba John, who lived near the city of Lycon in the Thebaïd, through the virtue of obedience was even given the grace of prophecy, and was so universally famed that his merits became well known even to the rulers of this world. For although as we have said he lived in the most remote region of the Thebaïd, the Emperor Theodosius never dared to proceed to war against his wicked enemies without taking advice of his foresight and hearing his answers. He would trust them as if he had heard them from heaven, and bring back trophies of victory from the most overwhelming foes.

Chapter 24 - Of the dry stick which the same Abba John did not cease to water at his superior's command as if it would grow.

The same Saint John served his novice-master from his youth until he was of full age, as long as the old man remained alive, and followed his commands with such humility that his obedience astounded even the superior himself. The latter wished to ascertain whether this virtue proceeded from true faith and a real simplicity of heart, or from affectation only, under duress, or for display before the superior, and so he often used to order him to do unnecessary, futile or even impossible things. I will give you three examples so you may have the opportunity of knowing how genuine was his heart and his obedience.

The old man took a stick from his woodbox, which had already been cut and got ready for the stove, and, since there had been no occasion to cook, it had become not just dry but was almost rotten through the passage of time. He stuck this into the ground before John, and ordered him to fetch water every day and irrigate it twice a day, so that through regular moistening it could take root and revive to its former growth, and its spreading branches would please the sight and provide shade in the summer's heat for those seated beneath it. The youth, with his usual devotion, took no consideration of the impossibility of the request, but carried it out daily, never failing to bring the water from about two miles away, and he never stopped watering the stick. For a whole year he allowed neither bodily illness, nor the celebration of a feast-day, nor any other necessary task to give him a legitimate excuse from carrying out the command; not even the harshness of winter was able to prevent him from obeying his orders. The old man silently and secretly watched him, diligent at his daily task, and observed how he obeyed his orders in simplicity of heart, as if they had come to him from God, without so much as a grimace or a grumble. Glad at his genuine and humble obedience, he took pity on his long labour, which he had fulfilled with such devotion for a whole year. He approached the dry stick and said "Oh, John, has this tree put out roots, or not?" When he said that he didn't know, the old man, as if investigating whether it was so, easily pulled out the stick in front of him as if testing whether the roots gave any resistance, and throwing it away ordered him to stop watering it henceforth.

Chapter 25 - How John threw away the only jar of oil at his master's command.
So it was that, trained by this sort of exercise, the youth grew daily in this virtue of obedience, and the grace of humility was seen in him, so that the sweet savour of his docility perfumed the monastery, as it were. Some of the brothers, wanting to test him or to be edified by him, went to the novicemaster and expressed their wonder at what they heard of his obedience. Suddenly the old man called him and

said "Go, and take the oil jar (the only one in that desert which served to provide any grease for themselves or their visitors) and throw it out of the window." He ran to carry out what his superior bade, and hurling it from the window smashed it on the ground, taking no thought nor consideration of the foolishness of the command, nor of the daily need, their bodily weakness, the waste of money or the poverty and inaccessibility of the desert in which, even if money were available, the lost material could not be found or replaced.

Chapter 26 - How Abba John obeyed his master when he tried to roll over a huge rock which not even many people would have been able to move.
Again, when others were seeking inspiration from his example of obedience, the old man called him, "Run, John," he said, "and roll that stone over here as soon as you can." He immediately attempted to roll over the rock, which was so big that a great crowd of men would be unable to shift it; he strained and forced it, now with his back, now with his whole weight. Sweat burst from every limb and not only soaked his clothing but even showed wet on the stone behind his shoulders. On this occasion too, he took no concern for the impossibility of performing the command, and in his reverence for his superior, and simple unfeigned obedience, trusted totally that his master would never give any order that was futile or meaningless.

Chapter 27 - Of the humility and obedience of Abba Patermutus, when he did not hesitate to throw his little boy into the river in obedience to the superior.
These few stories out of many about Abba John will be enough - now I will tell you something worth recording about Abba Patermutus. He was so eager to renounce this world, and remained lying at the gate of the monastery for so long that although it was quite against the custom of the monastery, his constant perseverance induced them to receive him along with his little son, who was about eight years old. Once they were finally received, they were at once entrusted to different novicemasters, and were put to live in separate cells, lest the father, seeing his dear child, might be reminded that only this son remained

of all the earthly cares and affections that he had renounced and abandoned. That he might be the more aware that he was no longer rich, he should not know that he was a father. To test him the more, and see if he would be more moved by family affection and the love of his own brood, than by the obedience and mortification of Christ, which every monk should prefer to his love, they deliberately neglected the child, dressed him in rags rather than clothes, and let him be so grubby and dishevelled that he might be more offensive than pleasing to his father's eyes whenever he caught sight of him. The child was even subjected to cuffs and slaps, which during his training the father saw some of them inflict on the innocent for no reason, so that he never saw him without his cheeks being marked by the signs of tears. Although he saw the child being treated like this day after day before his eyes, the father's feelings remained firm and unmoving, for the love of Christ and by virtue of obedience. He no longer considered him to be his son, for he had offered the child to Christ along with himself; he took no concern for his present injuries, but was rather glad that he saw them being borne, however uselessly; he thought little of the tears but was zealous for his own humility and perfection. The superior of the monastery, seeing how firm his mind was and how unwavering his determination, decided to test his strength of mind still further: one day when he noticed the child weeping, he pretended to be enraged at him, and ordered the father to pick him up and throw him in the Nile. The father, as if the command had been given him by Our Lord, at once ran and snatched up his son and carried him in his own arms to the river bank to throw him in. The deed would have been done, so strong was his trusting faith and obedience, had not some of the brethren been stationed in advance to watch the riverbank carefully; as the child was thrown they caught him, snatching him as it were from the river's maw. Thus they prevented the command, performed as it was by the father's obedience and devotion, from having any effect.

Chapter 28 - How it was revealed to an abbot that Abba Patermutus had

performed a sacrifice like Abraham's, and how the same Patermutus succeeded that
abbot in governing the monastery after his death.

His faith and devotion were so pleasing to God that they were given a
sign of divine approval. For it was revealed to a nearby superior that
he had performed this obedience like the Patriarch Abraham. When,
not long after, that same monastic superior went from this world's life
to Christ, he recommended to all the brothers that Patermutus be his
successor and abbot of the monastery.

Chapter 29 - Of the obedience of the brother who carried about ten baskets in
public, and distributed them at the abbot's command.

Nor should I pass over a brother, my own acquaintance, who was of
good birth according to the standards of this world, for his father was
a wealthy earl, and he was well educated in the liberal arts. When he
left his family to enter the monastery, he was immediately ordered by
the superior, to test how humble his mind and fervent his faith might
be, to take upon his shoulders ten baskets, which were not needed, and
sell them publicly, carrying them about in the streets for distribution.
He added this further condition, in order to keep him at this
employment longer, that if anyone should happen to want to buy
them all together, he should not permit it, but should sell them to the
enquirers one by one. He performed this with great diligence, and
scorned the shame and embarrassment of it in the name and for the
love of Christ. He took the baskets on his shoulders, sold them
separately at the agreed price, and brought the money to the
monastery. He was in no way deterred by the novelty of such a base
and unusual task, considering neither the indignity of the part, nor his
noble birth, nor the disadvantageous trade, since he longed to obtain,
through the grace of obedience, that lowliness of Christ which is true
nobility.

Chapter 30 - Of the humility of Abba Pinufius, who, in his desire for
mortification, left a famous monastery in which he was the presiding priest, and
sought a distant monastery in which he might be received as a novice.

The length of this book urges me to make an end, but the merit of obedience, which holds first rank among the other virtues, will not suffer me to pass over in silence the stories of those who were distinguished in this matter of humility. Steering a middle path, therefore, that is to say between brevity and the benefit requested by my enquirers, I will give one more example of humility, which was performed not by a novice but by an experienced superior, so that the reading of it may not only instruct juniors but even inspire seniors to the virtue of perfect humility. Abba Pinufius, with whom I was acquainted, was priest in a vast monastery in Egypt not far from the city of Panephysum. He was held by all in great esteem and veneration because of his own dignity as well as that of his profession, age and priesthood. He realised that this made it impossible for him to practice humility in the way in which he desired, nor to have any opportunity to exercise the virtue of subordination which he wanted, and so he secretly fled the monastery to dwell alone in the remotest region of the Thebaïd. There he put off his monastic habit and, dressed as a layman, made his way to the monastery of Tabenna which he knew to be the strictest of all. Here he believed he could be unknown because of the remoteness of the place, and hoped to be easily concealed in a large monastery among so many brothers. He persevered at the gate for a long time, knelt before all the brethren and begged them earnestly to receive him. Eventually they admitted him, but with great reluctance, thinking that a broken down old man who had lived all his life in the world and asked to enter a monastery in his old age would not have time enough left to overcome his passions, so that they suspected he was not interested in entering religion for that purpose but was driven by necessity, hunger and poverty. He was given charge of the garden, as an old man unfit for proper work. He laboured there under a younger brother who was put in charge of him, and was so docile to him, and cultivated the virtue of humility he longed for with such obedience that he diligently performed every day not only the necessary garden work but even all the tasks which others found difficult, undignified or generally to be shunned. Some chores he did by rising in the night in secret without anyone seeing or knowing, so that no one ever discovered who had done the work. Thus he lived there for three years, while his brethren spread all over the country looking for him, until a visitor from Egypt happened to spot him, although he could hardly recognise him in such a lowly dress and base employment. For he was bent under the weight of a hamper and was cultivating the earth for vegetables, manuring their roots with dung brought on his back. When the brother saw him, he remained long in doubt over recognising him, but finally approached him and examined his face carefully, listened to the sound of his voice, and threw himself straightway at his feet. This caused great astonishment among all those who saw it, who wondered why he should show this reverence to one who was considered the newest novice, freshly come from the world. They were further struck with amazement when he revealed the name which even they knew to be distinguished. Then all the brothers begged pardon for their previous ignorance, having placed him so long among the youths and novices, but he was aggrieved, and lamented that the devil's envy had cheated him of his worthy and humble way of life. For so long he had sought for it, and at last had gladly found it, but alas he had not succeeded in finishing his days in the lowliness he sought. They took him back to his own monastery, and watched him carefully lest he escape them again and slip away in the same manner.

Chapter 31 - How Abba Pinufius, brought back to his monastery and dwelling there for a little time, escaped once again into Syria.
When he had remained there a little while, he was struck again by the same desire and zeal for humility, and took advantage of the night silence to escape, heading this time not for a neighbouring province but for countries far off, unknown and foreign. He decided to go to Palestine, and took ship thither, thinking he would be better concealed if he escaped to regions where not even his name was known. Reaching Palestine he made for my own monastery which was not far from the cave in which Our Lord was pleased to be born of the

Virgin. Here he stayed a while, but in Our Lord's words, like a city
built on a mountain top (*Matth. 5:14*) he could not remain concealed.
For brothers from Egypt visited frequently for the sake of praying at
the Holy Places; they recognised him and drew him back to his
monastery with forceful entreaties.

*Chapter 32 - What advice the same Abba Pinufius gave to a brother whom he
received into his monastery in our presence.*
After this we went to seek him out in Egypt, because of the
admiration which we had conceived for the old man while he stayed in
our monastery. I think I should include in my text the advice which
he gave to a brother whom he received into his monastery in our
presence, for I believe much profit may be gained by this. "You
know", he said, "how many days you lay at the gates before being
received today. You should know at once what was the reason for that
delay. You can profit much in this life which you wish to embrace, if
you recognise its value, and thereby enter the service of Christ with
the right intentions."

*Chapter 33 - How great is the reward due to a monk who labours in the way of
the Fathers, but how great the penalty for failing, so that no one should be lightly
admitted into the community.*
Just as an immense reward of glory is promised for those who
faithfully serve God, and who adhere to the rule of this institute, in
the same way grievous penalties await those who are lukewarm and
careless in following the rule and fail to produce fruits of holiness
fitting for what they have professed or are believed by men to be. It
is better, as Scripture says, not to vow at all than to vow and fail to
fulfil, (*Eccles. 5:4*) and accursed is he who does the work of the Lord
carelessly. (*Jerem. 48:10*) That is why we refused for a long time to
accept you; it is not that we do not wholeheartedly desire to embrace
your salvation, or indeed any man's, and we are eager to run to meet
those who wish to be converted to Christ, however far off. However
if we received men lightly, we would run the risk of a light punishment

from God, but you of a heavy one; if you were too easily admitted now, without understanding the difficulty of this way of life, you would either stay with us unhappily, or desert us altogether. Therefore you must first understand why we kept you waiting, and once you have grasped that, you will more readily receive instruction on what you should do.

Chapter 34 - How our self-denial is nothing other than mortification in the image of the Crucified.

Self-denial is nothing other than the sign of mortification and bearing the cross. So that you may know this day that you are dead to this world and its works and desires, and that as the Apostle says (*Gal. 6:14*) you are 'crucified to this world, and the world to you', ponder well what the Cross brings, for under the banner of the Cross you will serve as long as the light lasts; for now 'it is not you that live but He lives in you who was crucified for you'. (*Gal. 2:20*) It is needful for us to pass through this world in the same garment and manner as he, when he hung upon the gibbet for us, as David sings: when we pierce our flesh through fear of the Lord, (*Psalm 118/9: 120*) let us have our whole desire and intention fixed not in the service of our own passions but on His mortification. Thus we shall fulfil the command of Our Lord, saying, (*Matth. 10:38*) 'He who does not take up his cross and follow me, is not worthy of me.' But perhaps you are wondering how a man can really carry his cross, or how he can have been crucified if he still lives. Hear the reason in brief:

Chapter 35 - That our Cross is the Fear of the Lord.

Our Cross is the Fear of the Lord. Just as one who is crucified has no longer the ability to move or turn his limbs as he wills, so we must adapt our will and desire not to pursue what is pleasant to us or delightful at the moment, but according to the law of the Lord who thus constrains us. Just as he who is fixed to the gibbet of the cross thinks no more of things present, nor considers his own desires, and is not concerned with the cares and worries of the next day, being moved by no possibility of seeing it, animated by no pleasure, no ambition, no pride; he does not grieve for his present sufferings nor remember those past, but though he still breathes in the body he knows himself to be beyond the use of all faculties, having in his heart only the knowledge that he is certainly to die - thus we too, crucified in the fear of the Lord, should be dead to all these things, that is not only fleshly vices but even their possibilities, keeping the eyes of our mind fixed there, where we must hope, from moment to moment, to pass away. In this manner we are able to keep all our fleshly desires and longings mortified.

Chapter 36 - That our self-denial is of no use if we are still entangled in the things we have denied.

Be careful, therefore, not to take up again any of the things which you have renounced and cast away. Do not, against the Lord's warning, (*Matth. 24:18*) turn back from the field of the Gospel to fetch your tunic, to be clothed again in what you had put off. Neither should you think about the base and earthly desires and concerns of this world, and against Christ's command descend from the housetop of perfection, and presume to pick up any of those things which you have renounced and left. (*ibid., 17*) Beware of remembering your family and your former friends, beware being called back to the worries of this age, putting your hand to the plough and, as the Saviour says, looking back, to become unfit for the kingdom of heaven. (*Luke 9:62*) Beware of the pride which you are now trampling underfoot, being at the beginning full of faithful zeal and humility, lest when you become bored with chanting psalms and every detail of our way of life, you become elated and find pride rising again, so that you rebuild what you have thrown down, as the Apostle says, (*Gal. 2:18*) and make yourself a renegade. No - remain even to the end in that nakedness which you have promised before God and his angels. Let that humility and patience in which you begged us to receive you into the monastery, remaining outside the gates for ten days of copious tears, let that not only persist but even grow and flourish in you. For it would be a tragic thing that when you ought to be advancing from your simple beginnings and aspiring to perfection, you might actually begin to decline from that state to a worse. For it is not he who begins this work who will be saved, but he who perseveres in it even to the end. (*Matth. 24:13*)

Chapter 37 - How the Devil is always eager for our destruction, and how we must ever be on the watch for his head.

The subtle serpent watches ever for our heels, (*Gen. 3:15*) that is he plots our destruction and strives to overthrow us at the end of our life. It is therefore of no avail to have begun well, nor to have embraced the first stages of renunciation with great fervour, unless they are followed and concluded by a fitting end; let the humble poverty of Christ, which you are now professing before Him, be preserved by you even to the end of your life in the same manner in which you began. That you may be able to fulfil this, be ever watchful for the Devil's heads, that is to say the first stirrings of thought, and bring them quickly before your novice master. Thus you will learn to crush the first movements of temptation, as long as you are never ashamed to reveal them all to your master.

Chapter 38 - Of the monk's preparation for meeting temptation, and how few are fit to be imitated.

And so, as you prepare to serve the Lord, be firm in the fear of the Lord, as Scripture says, (*Ecclus. 2:1*) and make yourself ready not for repose, security and pleasure, but for trials and difficulties. For it is through many tribulations that we must enter the Kingdom of God. (*Acts 14:21*) Narrow is the gate and strait the way that leads to life, and few there are who find it. (*Matth. 7:14*) Let yourself be influenced by a few chosen men, and let not the example of the careless multitude cool your zeal. Live like the few, so that with the few you may be found worthy of the Kingdom of God. For many are called, but few are chosen. (*Matth. 20:16*) It is a small flock to which the Father was pleased to grant an inheritance. (*Luke 12:32*) Do not therefore consider it a slight fault, if one who has promised perfection should go after things which are less than perfect. It is by the following stages and process that you may come to this point of perfection:

Chapter 39 - The steps by which we should mount to perfection, and the gradual ascent from the Fear of God to perfect Charity.

The Fear of the Lord, as I have said, is the beginning of our salvation and its safeguard. Through this it is that we may achieve our first conversion, the reform of our life, the protection of our virtue, as we set out on the way of perfection. When this fear penetrates the mind of a man, it begets a contempt for all things, and brings to birth forgetfulness of family and a revulsion from this world; for humility is gained through despising and setting aside all created things. Humility may be detected by these signs: firstly, if we have mortified all our desires; secondly if we conceal nothing from our master not only of our actions but even of our thoughts; thirdly if we act never at our own will but at our master's bidding, listening to his commands eagerly and willingly; fourthly if we preserve at all times obedience, docility and endurance; fifthly if we not only refrain from injuring others, but bear injury ourselves without grieving or complaining; sixthly if we do nothing on our own initiative but follow the common rule and the general custom; seventhly if we be content with the lowest position, and consider ourselves lazy and unworthy servants in all our responsibilities; eighthly if we do not merely profess with our lips that we be inferior to all others, but really believe it in our hearts; ninthly if we restrain our tongue and never shout aloud; tenthly if we be not easily moved to laughter. True humility may be detected by these signs and others like them, and when it is possessed in truth it will swiftly bring you to that charity which drives out fear. At this level of excellence all these things which at first you observed out of fear of punishment, you may now embrace quite naturally and without effort. No longer will you be moved by the recollection and dread of suffering, but by the love of goodness in itself and joy in virtue.

Chapter 40 - How a monk should not seek for a pattern of perfection among many but from one or but a few.

In order to arrive more quickly at this state, you should look among those dwelling in the community for examples of perfect life to imitate, but from few of them, perhaps one or two, not many. Besides the fact that few can be found who have amended their lives and refined them to real purity, it is also more helpful to be inspired and more efficient to be formed by the example of one man in attaining that perfection, which is the monastic life.

Chapter 41 - How those who live in the monastery should take on the semblance of disabilities.

There are three things necessary for you to observe in our congregation in order to attain this and to persevere for ever under the spiritual rule - as the Psalm says, 'I was like the deaf man who heard not, like the dumb who opened not his mouth; I am become like a man who hears nothing, in whose mouth is no defence.' *(Psalm 37/8:14-15)* You too should begin as if you were deaf, dumb and blind, so that apart from observing the one who was chosen for you to not. If you or any of your associates are wronged, stand firm, and listen like the dumb to the threat of retaliation, keeping this verse of the Psalms always in mind, 'I said, I will guard my ways and I will not sin with my tongue. I have placed a guard over my lips when the sinner stands up against me, I was dumb and was humiliated, and kept silent from good things'. *(Psalm 38/9:2-3)* And there is a fourth thing to cultivate above all, which will adorn and approve the three we have mentioned, that is to make yourself a fool in this world that you may become wise, as the Apostle says. *(I Cor. 3:18)* Take no consideration or assessment of what is commanded you, but give obedience always with a totally simple faith, considering only that to be holy, useful or wise which is ordained for you by the law of God or the superior's command. If you are trained in this way, you may endure under this rule for ever, and neither the enemy's temptations nor his counsels can wrest you from the monastery.

Chapter 42 - That a monk should not hope to attain patience from the strength of others but from his own perseverance.

Do not hope to attain patience from the strength of others, meaning that you will achieve it only when no one irritates you - that can never happen, and is beyond your power - but rather from your own humility and perseverance, which does depend on your own will.

Chapter 43 - A recapitulation of how a monk may rise to perfection.

Now in order to fix in your memory what I have described in this long sermon, so that it may remain embedded in your heart, I will make a brief summary, so that you may include the whole matter in the compass of a few short points. So listen briefly to the order in which you may quite easily rise to the heights of perfection. As Scripture says, the first stage of our salvation and our wisdom is the fear of the Lord. (*Prov. 1:7*) From fear of the Lord rises a saving compunction. From heartfelt compunction rises self-denial, that is being naked and spurning all material things. From this nakedness rises humility. From humility is born mortification of the will. By mortification of the will all vices are uprooted and wither away. Once vices are removed, virtues may grow and bear fruit. Through the abundance of virtues is attained purity of heart. By purity of heart we may possess the perfection of Apostolic charity.

THE EIGHT DEADLY SINS

BOOK FIVE

Of the Spirit of Greed

Chapter 1 - Transition from monastic training to the struggle against the eight deadly sins.

With God's help we proceed to the fifth book. After four little books concerned with the training of monks, we now arrive, as you have requested, at the struggle against the eight deadly sins, which we shall describe as the Lord gives us strength. Namely, the first is greed, understood as gluttony; the second irregular sexuality; the third is avarice, understood as greed or even lust for money; the fourth is wrath; the fifth melancholy; the sixth depression, which is anxiety or listlessness of heart; the seventh vainglory, meaning silly or frivolous conceit; the eighth is pride. As we begin to tackle this challenge, according to your request, blessed Pope Castor, we shall need to examine what these vices are, looking carefully into the smallest and most obscure details, then we can adequately explain how they arise, and finally be able to prescribe suitable remedies to cure them.

Chapter 2 - How the roots of sin are found in everyone, generally unnoticed, so that we need the Lord's help to discover them.

The roots of these passions should be clearly known to everyone, for they were revealed in the teaching of the elders, but since every one of us is ravaged by them and they are inborn in every one, we must begin by uncovering them. I would gain confidence that I could explain them to some extent if you were to pray that the prophecy of Isaiah were to be fulfilled in me: "I will go before you, I will humble the powerful of the earth, I will break the doors of bronze and shatter the bars of iron; I will open to you hidden treasures and the deepest secrets." (*Isaiah 45:2-3*) We are guided by the word of God; let him first humble the powerful of the earth, that is those evil passions against which we strive, which exercise their dominion and relentless hold over our mortal bodies; let the Lord make them bow before our searching gaze; let him burst the gates of our ignorance and shatter the bars of vice which exclude us from true knowledge; let him lead us to the deepest secrets, and as the Apostle says, (*I Cor. 4:5*) let him reveal to our enquiry things which are hidden in darkness, and make known the thoughts of our hearts. Thus may we with clean hearts penetrate the darkness of vice, open it up and bring it out into the light. Let us be able to expound the roots and natures of sins, both to those who are free from them and those still enchained. Thus may our minds, according to the prophecy, (*Psalm 65/6:12*) pass through the fire of sin which scorches them so sorely, and swiftly plunge on, unscathed, into the waters of virtue which will cool them. Sprinkled with holy remedies, may we be found worthy to emerge with purity of heart into the cool repose of perfection.

Chapter 3 - How our first struggle is against the spirit of greed, that is gluttony.
The first round of our contest is against greed, which we can call gluttony. First we shall look at the subject of fasting and the quality of our food, and then turn to the rules and traditions of the Egyptians, since all are aware that they have the best discipline of self-control and a perfect system of understanding.

Chapter 4 - The evidence of Abba Anthony, which shows how one who possesses this can hope for every virtue.
Ancient and admirable is the teaching of Saint Anthony, that a monk who has once experienced the common life and strives to scale the summits of a greater perfection, and, after his motives have been carefully scrutinised, is able to rely on his own discretion in proceeding to the fastness of a hermitage, should never expect to find every type of virtue in any one man however exalted. For one man blooms with knowledge, another has a great reputation for discernment, another is solidly tolerant and patient; one is distinguished for humility, another for self-control, while another is striking for his noble simplicity. Yet

another stands out from the rest for greatness of mind, another for works of mercy, another for watchfulness, another for silence, another for hard work. Hence if a monk wants to bear the fruits of monastic spirituality, he should, like a sagacious bee, collect the nectar of each virtue from him who holds it dearest, and store it in the cells of his heart. Let him not trouble about lesser matters but ponder on how to gather each virtue, and how to make them bear fruit. Indeed if we wanted to acquire all of them from one man, such a model for our imitation could scarcely be found if at all. As the Apostle says, we do not even find that Christ himself did everything in all matters, but in this way we can find him as it were divided among many. For it is said of him, that he became for us the wisdom, the justice, the holiness and the redemption of God. (*I Cor. 1:30*) And since we find wisdom in one man, justice in another, holiness in a third, in others meekness, chastity, humility and patience, Christ is now divided up among each of our saints member by member. When all agree on one faith and one virtue, Christ returns as the perfect man, making up the fullness of his body (*Eph. 4:12*) in the particular virtues of each of his members. And so until that day come when God shall be all in all, in the meantime he can be God in all through this division of virtues, in the way we have described, even though he is not yet all in all in fullness of these virtues. Our religious life has but one end, but we come to God by many paths, as we shall see more fully in the Collations of the Fathers. We should therefore expect to find our models of discernment and continence particularly among those whom we notice to be most fruitful in displaying them, through the Holy Spirit. No one man can acquire all of what is distributed among many, but we should attempt to imitate those who most display the virtues of which we are capable.

Chapter 5 - That a common rule of fasting cannot be observed by all.
When it comes to fasting, it is not easy to observe a common discipline, since our physical strength varies, and such strength cannot be produced by sheer will-power, as in the case of other virtues. It is

because it does not depend on mental effort alone but requires the cooperation of the body, that we have come to agree on the following rule which was handed down to us: the time, manner and quantity of food should be varied according to physical strength, age and sex, whereas all alike can observe a common rule of self-denial to strengthen the mind and steel the soul. Not everyone is able to prolong the fast all week, but they can put off eating for three days or perhaps two. Many, enfeebled through sickness, or particularly through old age, cannot even endure to fast one day until sundown without great discomfort. Not for all is it enough to eat steeped vegetables, nor can everyone endure to live on nothing but leeks, and it is not universally acceptable to eat dry bread. One man may find that he can eat two pounds of bread without feeling full, whereas another may be glutted with one pound or even six ounces. Nevertheless there is one goal in mind, that no one should be sated and burdened with having eaten his fill. It is not just the quality of food but also its quantity which can blunten the point of the soul, and when the mind is fattened with the flesh it kindles a dangerously fiery spark of vice.

Chapter 6 - How the mind can be drunk on more than wine.
The belly generates the seeds of vice, with whatever food it is filled, and the mind is unable to moderate its choices if it is weighed down by much eating. It is not only the fumes of wine that inebriate the mind, but an excess of any food makes it fickle and feeble, and spoils it for any contemplation of pure virtue. It was not excessive drinking that led to the downfall of the licentious men of Sodom, but an excess of bread. Listen to the Lord speaking through the prophet in rebuke of Jerusalem: "How indeed did your sister Sodom fall? Was it not that she ate her bread in excess and abundance?" (*Ezek. 16:49*) Since through this surfeit of bread they became enflamed with irresistible carnal passion, they were burned up in fiery sulphur at God's decree. (*Gen. 19*) So if it was an excess of mere bread that drove them to such immorality through the sin of over-eating, what shall we say of those

who stuff their living bodies with such an unreasonable quantity of meat and wine, acting not to satisfy hunger but to consume as much as the whim takes them?

Chapter 7 - How bodily weakness is no hindrance to a pure soul.
The needs of the flesh are no hindrance to purity of heart, if we consume only what our bodily weakness requires, not what the appetite demands. We can observe that those who totally abstain from the richer types of food, rather than accepting them in moderation out of necessity, and deny themselves totally through longing for self-control, are more liable to fall than those who take whatever food their weakness needs, and keep to a moderate amount. [*We follow Migne's text here*] Bodily frailty has its own reward of continence, as long as we restrain ourselves while we are still hungry for the nourishing food we allow ourselves, and accept as much food as on careful consideration would be enough to live on, without giving in to what greed demands. More appetising food which promotes physical health does not hinder bodily purity if taken in moderation. Indeed whatever we eat for the sake of nourishment is used up in averting illness and exhaustion. Hence we need not be deprived of the virtue of restraint whatever the state of our health, as long as we do not eat as much as we feel like.

Chapter 8 - How food should be taken with the aim of perfect self-control.
The opinion of the Fathers is very true and admirable, that the standard of fasting and self-denial depends on moderation in abstinence and penance. The common goal of perfect virtue for all is that in eating the food which we need to sustain our bodies, we check ourselves while still hungry. No matter how frail someone may be physically, he can acquire as much virtue as the sturdy and healthy, if he mortifies the mental desires which his weak body is incapable of fulfilling. St Paul says, (*Rom 13:14*) "do not worry about the body and its urgings." He is not totally prohibiting care for the body, but prevents us from giving in to its passions. He prohibits luxurious pampering of the flesh, but does not exclude necessary care for life.

The former, lest we tumble into vile and passionate practices through pandering to the flesh; the latter lest the body, weakened by our fault, be unable to carry out its necessary and religious work.

Chapter 9 - Of moderation in penance, and the restraint of fasting.
The perfection of self-control is not only found in our use of time, nor the quality of our food, but is to be sought before the tribunal of conscience. For each one of us should set himself a target of self-denial adequate to the struggle against bodily frailty. The degree of fasting laid down by law is beneficial and should be kept by all, but unless that is followed by a reasonable meal, it is of no avail in the quest for holiness. For a long period of eating nothing at all, followed by eating as much as we like, is much more likely to make us sluggish rather than pure and chaste. Holiness of mind does go with an empty stomach, but you cannot achieve lasting chastity without being content to observe a reasonable moderation. No matter how strict the fasting, if it is followed by over indulgence, it is useless, and much more likely to lead to the sin of gluttony. It is better to eat a sensible amount every day than to keep occasional severe prolonged fasts. Unreasonable fasting has been known not only to weaken the will, but even to make it impossible to pray, when the body is so enfeebled.

Chapter 10 - Abstinence from food is not enough to ensure purity in mind and body.
Abstinence from food alone is not enough to preserve the integrity of mind and body, unless the other virtues of the soul be added. Humility must be learnt first, through the practice of obedience, heartfelt contrition and bodily labour. We must not only repudiate the ownership of money, but even root out the very desire of it. Simply not being rich is not enough, for many are in that state out of necessity, but we should not even be willing to accept wealth that happens to be offered. Then we must eliminate wrath and overcome melancholy, spurn vainglory (that is conceit) and trample pride underfoot, restraining the wandering mind and its irregular thoughts

by constant recollection of God. The mirky meanderings of the mind must be called back into the contemplation of God as often as our subtle foe slips such ideas into our secret thoughts, striving to capture our minds by this means.

Chapter 11 - Bodily desires are not extinguished except by stamping out vice.
Now it is impossible to extinguish the desires of our hearts before the germs of other principal vices are eradicated: if God wills we will speak about each of these in turn in separate books. Here our concern is with gluttony, greed for food, which is the first thing to be overcome. He who is unable to restrain the pangs of gluttony will never be able to check the burning arrows of desire. Interior chastity is marked by the perfection of this virtue. You will never find one who is defeated by weakness in the easiest of struggles able to hold his own in the more severe conflict. For all virtues have something in common, however many types and names we may distinguish, just as gold is a single element no matter how varied the many types of jewellery are that the skilled goldsmith may decide to make. So it is that one who is found wanting in any part of virtue cannot possess the whole. How can we believe that someone has extinguished the burning darts of lust, which are kindled not by the body's motions alone but also by mental habits, if he has been unable to control the pricks of anger which arise from the heart alone? Or how could we imagine one who simply cannot overcome the vice of pride being able to blunt the lustful arrows of body and mind? How can you trust someone to trample underfoot inborn fleshly urges if he cannot restrain the lure of money which is an external thing, not part of our own nature? Is it reasonable to suppose that you can win the war against flesh and blood if you cannot heal the sickness of melancholy? No matter how great a city is, defended by high walls and strongly barred gates, if one tiny postern is betrayed, it will be sacked. What difference does it make if the destroying foe makes his way into the city over high walls and in through wide gates, or through a narrow and secret passage?

Chapter 12 - How the spiritual struggle should imitate secular games.

He who competes in the games is not rewarded unless he contends correctly. (*II Tim. 2:5*) He who wants to extinguish the natural appetites of the flesh must first be eager to overcome vices which are beyond nature. If we wish to experience the force of the Apostle's words we must first get to know the laws and customs of worldly competitions, so that by comparison with them, in the spiritual conflict, we may know what the holy Apostle wanted us to learn from this example. In those games in which the victors win a crown that fades, as St Paul puts it, it is customary for him who gets ready to compete for the coveted wreath, which carries with it the privilege of legal immunity, and who desires to win the supreme prize in the games, first to display his youthful strength in the elementary competitions, in the Olympic or Pythian Games. In these the younger ones who want to compete in these events are adjudicated both by the President of the Games and by the whole crowd, to see whether they are fit to be allowed to compete. Each one is carefully examined, firstly to see if there be anything disreputable in his life; then they consider whether he be base-born in slavery and hence unworthy of the competition, or of associating with those who take part; then whether he can show proofs of skill and strength. Competing with those younger then he, or of the same age, if he demonstrates both skill and youthful prowess, then the President may decide to promote him from the colts' division to compete with grown men of real experience. Then if he can consistently hold his own against them in competition, as well as often winning trophies of victory among them, then at last he may deserve to compete in the great games, in which those alone may take part who have won prizes and have been rewarded with many wreaths. Now, knowing the structure of worldly competitions, by comparison with them we can understand what should be the discipline and structure of the spiritual conflict.

Chapter 13 - How, until we be freed from gluttony, we cannot begin the struggle of the inner man.

We should first demonstrate our freedom from subjection to the flesh. For "a man is a slave to that which overcomes him", (*II Pet. 2:19*) and "all who commit sin, are slaves". (*John 8:34*) When the President of the Games examines us and finds us untainted by the reputation of foul vice, and that we are not to be eliminated as baseborn slaves to the flesh, unfit for the Olympic struggle against sin, then we may begin the contest against those born with us, that is the desires of the flesh and the disturbed motions of the soul. It is impossible for a bloated belly to cope with the struggles of the inner man, nor can one who is liable to fall at the first trial be fit to engage in more serious warfare.

Chapter 14 - How gluttony may be defeated.
That is why we must begin by crushing gluttony, and the mind be stretched not only by fasting, but by watching, reading and frequent examination of conscience, when we remember our past temptations and falls, groaning with the horror of sin, and igniting a desire for perfection and integrity. Once the mind is occupied and interested in these considerations, it will perceive the taking of food to be not so much giving in to desire as an obligation taken on like a burden, and will consider it to be more a matter of bodily necessity than mental delight. Once we have embraced this consideration with genuine compunction, we may resist the desires of the flesh and its burning arrows, which grow more demanding when overfed. Thus, by copious tears and heartfelt sighs, we may extinguish the furnace of the body, which is enkindled as if by the King of Babylon to create occasions of sin and habits of vice, burning us quite as much as brimstone and pitch. Then God's grace, which the Holy Spirit distils like a dew into our hearts, is able to soothe and quench the heats of carnal longing.

So that is our first trial, our first probation, as in the Olympic Games, to extinguish the lure of gluttony in our desire for perfection. For this reason the excessive desire for food is crushed by the consideration of virtue, to the extent that we take food with some anxiety as if it were a natural necessity but contrary to chastity. Eventually we get into a way of life wherein we consider that for our spiritual concerns, no time is more difficult than that which we are obliged by our weakness to spend in looking after the body. And while we are constrained by this necessity, concerned more with keeping alive than with our real intentions, we are eager to get away from what hinders our work of salvation as quickly as possible. We would be quite unable to spurn the delight of earthly food had not our minds been fixed on pondering the things of God, and our joy even more in the love of virtue and the beauty of heaven. So it is that we can ignore the passing things of this world, since the mind is attentive to what is permanent and everlasting, and while still in the flesh, our hearts can contemplate the bliss of our life to come.

Chapter 15 - How a monk must be always intent on preserving purity of heart.
It is like one who seeks the great prizes for athletics: he is swift to strike, his keen eyesight following the javelin to the far off target which he can only just see; for he knows that a great and glorious reward and prize awaits him if he hit it. Hence he must keep his eyes on the target, looking at nothing else, for there he sees the supreme prize to be located. He will certainly miss the reward of skill and strength if his concentration diverges from it for a moment.

Chapter 16 - How a monk, imitating the Olympic contestants, cannot win the spiritual conflict until he has won against the flesh.
Now once the lure of gluttony has been overcome by this concentration, and we are declared to be free from slavery to the flesh, and untainted by vice, as in the Olympic Games we may be adjudged fit to compete with those senior to ourselves. Once these preliminaries are past, we can be entrusted with the conflict against spiritual foes, which is not fitting save for conquerors who are ready to compete in this divine struggle. This is the most fundamental principle in all our efforts, that the fleshly desires be first quenched. No one who has not gained control of his own body can compete legitimately. And unless his competition is legitimate, he can certainly not hold his own in the struggle, nor win any prize or gain the grace

of victory. If we fail in this contest, caught out like slaves to the lusts of the flesh, and unable to offer proof of freedom or strength, we shall be disgraced and eliminated from the conflict against the spirit as unworthy varlets. For "he who commits sin is a slave to it" (*John 8:34*), and St Paul speaks of those of whom fornication is reported, "the temptation which assails you is merely human." (*I Cor. 10:13*) We will not deserve to attain mental strength and take part in the more serious battle against spiritual evil, if we be incapable of controlling the weak flesh which opposes the spirit. Some have misunderstood St Paul and substituted the optative for the indicative, as to say "may no temptation more than human assail you", but it is clear that he really means to express not a desire but a statement or even a rebuke.

Chapter 17 - How the first foundations of the spiritual conflict are laid in the struggle against greed.

Do you want to know how the true athlete of Christ competes legitimately in the struggle? "I do not run", he says, "without a goal; I do not box, as if hitting the air; I punish my body and force it to obey, lest though preaching to others I myself be rejected." (*I Cor. 9:26-7*) See how he lays the basis of the struggle on the firm foundation of his own self, that is in the flesh, and begins his training by punishing the body and subduing his own flesh. "For I do not run without a goal." It is not without a goal, for he sees the heavenly Jerusalem and keeps that as a fixed goal for the unwavering determination of his heart. He does not run without a goal, for he forgets what is behind and strains towards the future, pursuing "the promised prize of God's sublime call, in Christ Jesus; (*Phil. 3:14*) ever there fixing the eyes of his mind, he rushes towards Him with heartfelt effort, and confidently exclaims, "I have fought the good fight, I have finished the race, I have kept the faith." Since he acknowledges that he has run tirelessly on the winged feet of conscience following the savour of Christ's anointing, and gained victory in the spiritual combat through chastising the flesh, he mounts the podium with confidence saying: "For the future there is laid up for me the crown of righteousness, which the Lord, the just Judge, will render to me on that day." To offer a similar hope of reward for us as well, if we are prepared to imitate him in running this race, he adds, "Not for me alone, but for all who love his presence"; (*II Tim. 4:7-8*) he declares that we shall share in his glory in the day of judgement, and we shall be victorious in the contest if we subdue the body, if we love the presence of Christ - not merely that presence when he will appear even to those who refuse him, but his daily presence when he visits his holy ones. The Lord speaks of this presence in the Gospel : "I and my Father will come to him and we shall dwell with him", (*John 14:23*) and again "Behold I stand at the door and knock: if anyone hear my voice and open the door I will go in to him and eat with him, and he with me." (*Apoc. 3:20*)

Chapter 18 - How many are the kinds of contests and prizes through which the Apostle rose to the supreme crown in the games.

It is not only the running event that St Paul claims to have completed; when he says "I do not run without a goal", this particularly refers to the intention and fervour in which his spirit followed Christ wholeheartedly, singing with the Bride: "Let us run after you in the savour of your anointing," (*Cant. 1:3*) and again, "My soul clings to you"; (*Psalm 62/3:9*) but he also claims to have won other types of competition, when he says "I do not box as if hitting the air, but I punish my own body and force it to obey." (*I Cor. 9:26-7*) This really means the effort of self-control, physical fasting and mortifying the flesh; he calls himself a boxer strong against his own flesh, who strikes blows against it, blows of self-control which are not fruitless, for he won the boxing prize by subduing his body. Once toughened by these blows of self-control, and bruised by the gloves of fasting, he confers on his victorious spirit the crown of immortality and the palm of incorruption. Here you see the proper programme for the games, and can see the result of the spiritual contest: for Christ's athlete, victorious against rebel flesh, is carried in as the supreme champion with subdued flesh trampled beneath his feet. He "does not run without a goal", since he trusts he will straightway enter the holy city, the heavenly Jerusalem. He boxes, by fasting and bodily mortification, "not as if hitting the air", launching blows of self-control fruitlessly; by subduing the body he strikes not the empty air but the spirits that inhabit it. When he says "not as if hitting the air", he means that he is striking something in the air, not the empty and unresisting air itself. Since he has been victorious in these events and made his entry enriched with the proceeds of many prizes, he is found worthy to begin the contest against more formidable foes, and after triumphing over the first competitors, he is confident in proclaiming, "Our contest now is not against flesh and blood but against principalities and powers, against the rulers of darkness in this world, against the spirits of wickedness in the heavens." (*Eph. 6:12*)

Chapter 19 - How Christ's athlete, while he remains in the body, does not cease from the fight.
There will never come an end of prizes for competing as long as the athlete of Christ remains in the body. The greater and more successful he grows in triumph, the tougher the competition becomes. Once the flesh is subdued and conquered, how many ranks of foes, how many regiments of enemies are stirred up by his conquests to rise against the victorious soldier of Christ! There should certainly be no respite of peace for Christ's soldier to grow lazy and begin to forget the glorious struggles of his career, or to become slack in security and so be robbed of the prizes he has won and the glory he has earned. If we too wish to grow in strength and aspire to these levels of honour, we too should begin the struggle in the same order, starting with the Apostle's words "I do not box, as if hitting the air; I punish my body and force it to obey," (*I Cor. 9:26-7*) so that when we have won this event we can say, again in his words, "Our contest now is not against flesh and blood but against principalities and powers, against the rulers of darkness in this world, against the spirits of wickedness in the heavens." (*Eph. 6:12*) There is no other way in which we may compete with them, nor can we be fit to tackle the spiritual combat, if we are

defeated in the struggle with the flesh or knocked out in boxing against the belly. How rightly the Apostle exhorts us, saying, "The temptation which assails you is merely human." (*I Cor. 10:13*)

Chapter 20 - That a monk must not eat outside the usual time, if he wishes to qualify for the interior conflict.

That is why a monk who aspires to the interior conflict must first of all take this precaution, that he be not enticed by the enjoyment of any food or drink to indulge himself in partaking alone, away from the table, before the proper procession at the time for the common meal. Nor, when the meal is over, should he allow himself to take the least morsel. In the same way he should observe the statutory hours and period of sleep. By this practice the lusts of the mind are restrained, and sexual vice eliminated. For how could someone who is unable to restrain his appetite for extra food be capable of quenching the burning lusts of the flesh? And how could someone who cannot control desires that are public and petty, be sufficiently self-disciplined to defeat secret desires that no one would witness? Therefore strength of character can be tested on particular occasions and by any sort of temptation, for if he be conquered by trivialities in public, let his own conscience judge whether he will endure overwhelming temptatio n in private.

Chapter 21 - Of the inner peace of a monk, and of spiritual abstinence.

We do not have an external enemy to fear - our enemy is within ourselves. It is a civil war that rages inside us every day, but once we have conquered there, all external foes are reduced to nothing, and the soldier of Christ will have perfect peace and ease. There is no external foe to fear once we have overcome the spiritual rebel within. We do not consider that fasting from visible food is enough for a perfect heart and a pure body, unless a fasting of the soul be added to it. The soul too has dangerous foods and if it grows fat on them, even if they be not excessive, it can fall into the pit of lust. Detraction is its food, and how sweet it is! Wrath is its food, however mild it be. If you feed on that wretched fare even for an hour, you will be laid up by its poison. Envy is a food of the mind, which rots it with its virulent juice, and is enflamed by another's prosperity to leave you in ceaseless pain. Vainglory or conceit is its food, which for a time delights you with its taste, but leaves you afterwards empty, robbed of all virtue, stripped and incapable of any spiritual fruit. This food does not only deprive you of the merit of all your great labours, but even loads a greater penalty on you. Every sort of desire and fickle flight of fancy is food for the soul, which fill it with poisonous matter and deprive it henceforth of the real Bread of Heaven, the genuine nourishment. So if by a holy fast we do our best to abstain from these things, we will find our physical abstinence useful and agreeable. For work, coupled with mortification of the flesh, makes us a most acceptable sacrifice for God and a dwelling place for holiness, in every part pure and clean. If we fast physically but are wrapped up in malicious thoughts, our bodily mortification will be useless as long as our nobler part is corrupt, and we shall fail in that very area where we should be made dwelling places of the Holy Spirit. The house of God and dwelling place of the Holy Spirit is not found in perishable flesh but in a pure heart. That is why when the outer man fasts, the inner man should be likewise restrained from dangerous foods. The holy Apostle instructs us to exhibit ourselves clean for God, that we may be fit to receive Christ as a guest, in these words: "in the inner man let Christ dwell, through faith, in your hearts." (*Eph. 3:16-7*)

Chapter 22 - How we should practice bodily restraint so that we may arrive at spiritual fasting.

We have discovered that the reason for practising bodily restraint is that by this fasting we may attain purity of heart. We would have ceaseless trouble for the future if we undertook this fast incessantly, thinking of our goal, but were unable to attain that goal for the sake of which we have endured such affliction. It would be better to moderate the forbidden foods of the soul than to fast from the permitted and less dangerous foods of the body. The latter are God's simple creations which we may eat, and are themselves in no way sinful; but by the first of the former we actually devour our brethren, of which it is said: "Be not fond of detraction, lest you be uprooted," (*Prov. 20:13, LXX*) and the blessed Job says of anger and jealousy, "Wrath has slain the foolish, and jealousy has destroyed the little one." (*Job 5:2*) We should observe that the wrathful man is called foolish, and the jealous one a little one. Truly he may well be called foolish, who freely causes his own death under the stimulus of anger, and the one who is envious demonstrates how little and insignificant he is. For in the act of envy he bears witness that the one whose prosperity annoys him is greater than he.

Chapter 23 - What the monk's food ought to be like.
Food should be chosen not only to soothe the burning pangs of lust, still less to inflame them, but which is easy to prepare and which is readily available for a moderate price, and it should be held in common for the brothers' use. Now there are three types of gluttony: one is a compulsion to anticipate the regular time of eating; another is wanting to fill the stomach with excessive amounts of any sort of food; the third is delighting in the more delicate and rare dishes. A monk therefore must take threefold care against these: firstly he must wait for the proper time of meals; then he must not yield to overeating; thirdly he should be happy with any sort of common food. Consuming anything unusual or out of the ordinary was considered by the ancient fathers to be tainted with vainglory and ostentation. None of those whom we admire for wisdom and discernment, or who are marked out by Christ's grace as shining examples for our imitation, are known to have refused what was then considered the most common and cheapest sort of bread. And yet those who declined to follow this rule, and spurned dry bread, searching for beans, vegetables or fruit, are never found among the most perfect monks, and failed to acquire the grace of discernment and knowledge. They do not only forbid a monk to want unusual foods, and to let his way of life become public knowledge, lest he become vain and empty-

headed till he perish of conceit, but they also state that one should not lightly reveal the common routine of fasting to anyone, but should cover it up and conceal it as far as possible. When brothers visit they consider it better to show them an example of human affection than to reveal to them the discipline of self-control and daily routine. We should put before them not what we ourselves choose to desire or need, but what is needful for the travellers to rest or recover, and to do this gracefully.

Chapter 24 - How we noticed that in Egypt, when we arrived, they easily dispensed the daily fast.
When we left Syria, in the desire to learn the wisdom of the elders, and arrived in Egypt, we were astonished at the heartfelt welcome we received, in that they did not observe the usual rule of not eating until the set time of fasting was over, which was how we had been trained in Palestine. Wherever we went the daily routine was suspended (except for the general Wednesday and Friday fast). We asked one of the elders why they so readily dispensed the daily fast, and he replied "Fasting I can do always, but I cannot always have you with me as a departing guest. Moreover fasting, however useful or even necessary it may be, is but a voluntary sacrifice, whereas it is compulsory to perform works of charity. That is why I receive Christ in you, and must refresh him; and after entertaining you for the sake of his humanity, I can always compensate by a stricter fast later. For 'the children of the bridegroom cannot fast while the bridegroom is with them, but when he is taken away, then they will fast.'" (*Luke 5:34-5*)

Chapter 25 - Of one elder's self-restraint, who ate six times in such a manner that he remained hungry.
One of the elders, while he was entertaining me and urging me to eat a little, when I said I could not, replied: "I have already laid the table six times for different brothers who arrived, and I have encouraged all of them to eat, and done so with them, yet I am still hungry - and are you saying you cannot eat when this is your first meal?"

Chapter 26 - Of another elder, who never ate while alone in his cell.

We met another, living alone, who asserted that he never ate while alone, but that even if no brother came to his cell for all five weekdays, he assiduously put off eating until on Saturday or Sunday he came to the church to take part in the common worship, and found some pilgrim there whom he could afterwards take back to his cell to eat in company with him, not so much to sustain his body but for the sake of kindness towards that brother. And as they know how to dispense the daily fast easily when a brother arrives, so when he has gone they can compensate for the meals they allowed themselves for his sake by a stricter abstinence; for when they do take a little food they mortify themselves in self-control by reducing not just the amount of bread but also of sleep.

Chapter 27 - The boasts of Abba Paesius and Abba John

The Abba Paesius lived in a vast wilderness, and was visited by Abba John, superior of a great monastery with many monks, who asked him, his ancient friend, what he had been doing for the forty years since they last met, living alone with few contacts with other monks. "The Sun," he said, "never caught me eating." "Nor me," said the other, "in ill temper."

Chapter 28 - The notable boast which the same Abba John left as an example when he died.

When the same abbot was lying on his deathbed, and eager for death as for his journey home, the monks gathered around him and begged him to leave them something to remember as a sort of bequest, so that by following his counsel they might better come to the summit of perfection. He sighed and said "I have never done my own will, nor have I taught others to do what I had not first done myself."

Chapter 29 - Of Abba Machetes who never fell asleep during spiritual conferences, but always did so when earthly tales were told.

We met an elder called Machetes, who was distinguished from the majority by his way of life, and had long entreated the Lord for this favour, that whenever spiritual conferences took place, by day or by night, he might never be overcome by drowsiness, but if anyone presumed to utter a word against charity or something frivolous, he would straightway fall asleep, so that the poison of ill speech could not even reach so far as to touch his ears.

Chapter 30 - How the same elder considered no one should be judged.

The same elder when he was instructing us to judge no one, told us that there were three occasions on which he had checked or rebuked the monks, namely because many had had their tonsils cut out, because they had military greatcoats in their cells, and because they had blessed oil and given it to laypeople. He said he himself was guilty of all these. For when he was suffering from tonsillitis, as he said, "I suffered from this for so long that I allowed them to be cut out driven as much by pain as by the advice of all the elders. And because of this illness I was compelled to have a greatcoat. As for blessing oil and giving it to those who wanted it (which I was particularly opposed to, considering that it arose from great arrogance), once when a crowd of laymen suddenly surrounded me I was so pressed that I could not get away from them, and they compelled me with considerable violence to make the sign of the cross with my hand over the vase of oil they held out, but once they believed that they had got me to bless the oil, they let me go. And so I realised by this that if a monk be so rash as to rebuke others, he will himself fall into the same type of sin." Therefore each of us must judge himself alone, and always take great care and precautions never to discuss anyone else's way of life, as the Apostle commands: "Why do you judge your brother? Let him stand or fall before his own Lord." (*Rom. 14:10 and 4*) And again, "Judge not, that you be not judged, for in that judgement you judge, you yourselves shall be judged." (*Matth. 7:1-2*) And apart from the reason we have given, it is dangerous to judge others because we do not know what compulsion, what reason they have for doing what offends us, whether it be justified in God's eyes, or easily pardonable, so that we find ourselves making rash judgements, committing thereby a serious sin in thinking of our brothers other than as we ought.

Chapter 31 - How a certain elder rebuked the monks when he found them asleep during spiritual conferences, but alert when idle tales were told.

It was the same elder who said that the devil was the author of idle tales, and the constant foe of spiritual conferences, and proved it thus. When some of the brothers were discussing necessary and spiritual matters, he observed that they were sunk in forgetful slumber, and were unable to shake the pressure of sleep from their eyes; so he suddenly introduced a frivolous story. As he told it he saw them suddenly roused, pricking up their ears, and with a sigh he said, "Just now we were talking about heavenly matters, and your eyes were all heavy with forgetful slumber, but when an idle tale was introduced we all woke up and shook off that drowsiness. Learn from this, therefore, who is the foe of spiritual conversations, and the promoter of futile and earthly ones. It is abundantly clear that it is he who rejoices in evil, and never ceases to promote worldly conversation and stifle the spiritual."

Chapter 32 - Of the letters, burnt before they were read.

I think I ought also to recall this story about a brother, determined on purity of heart, and really earnest for the contemplation of God: when after fifteen years a number of letters were brought to him from his father and mother, and many friends from the province of Pontus, he took the great bundle of letters, and pondered long over them. "What a lot of thoughts would be roused in me by reading these, which would move me either to frivolous joy or fruitless grief! For how many days would the memory of the writers distract me from my heart's desire of contemplation! How long it would take to settle this disturbance of mind, how much effort it would need to restore my state of calm, if my mind were once aroused by reading these letters, by remembering their speech, their faces, which I have left behind so long - and again to feel the desire of seeing them once more, of living among them! Indeed it would be of no avail to have left them physically if my heart began to regard them again, and if the memory, which I renounced on leaving this world, as if dying, were to be again revived and admitted." Thinking this over, he decided not to open a single letter, not even to untie the bundle, lest he remember the names of the writers, or recall their faces and fall away from his spiritual purpose. So he handed the bundle over to be burnt, still tied up as he received it. "Go," he said, "thoughts of my fatherland! Be burnt up together, do not dare to call me back again to the things I have escaped!"

Chapter 33 - Of how Abba Theodore in prayer gained an answer to his question.
We met Abba Theodore, a man endowed with great holiness and wisdom, not only about daily life but also about sacred Scripture, which he acquired not through learned study or secular literary criticism, but through purity of heart alone. Indeed he could hardly understand or speak more than a few words of Greek. When he was puzzling over the meaning of some difficult point, he would spend seven days and nights in constant prayer, until he knew the answer to the problem through divine revelation.

Chapter 34 - Of the same elder's method of teaching a monk to acquire knowledge of Scripture.
When some of the brothers in admiration of his outstanding knowledge, were asking him the meaning of some passage in Scripture, he said: "If a monk wants to learn to understand Scripture, he should not waste his effort over books of commentaries, but instead he should direct all his mental and spiritual powers to eradicating carnal vices. Once these are cleared away from the mind's eye, and the veil of passion is lifted, he will begin to understand the secrets of Scripture as if by instinct. Indeed they were not given us by the Holy Spirit in order to be unknown or obscure, but they have become obscure because the eyes of our minds are clouded by a veil of sins, through our own fault. Once we are restored to our natural state of health, the mere reading of Holy Scripture will be quite

enough to understand true wisdom, and we shall have no need to learn from commentaries. In the same way our physical eyes need no instruction in how to see, as long as they are free from cataract or glaucoma. Now that is why so many mistakes and errors have arisen among the commentators themselves, because many of them have taken no care about purifying the mind, but rushed into interpretation, opining in their sluggish and unclean minds many things contrary to the faith, or to Scripture itself, and unable to grasp the light of truth.

Chapter 35 - How the same elder rebuked me when he came to my cell at midnight. The same Theodore came unexpectedly to my cell during a stormy night, to investigate with fatherly interest what I, who was new to the hermit life, was doing. He found me tired after the evening devotions, resting my body and lying on my rush mat. He sighed deeply and called me by name: "How many of us, dear John, are conversing with God at this moment! They embrace Him within themselves, and guard Him, while you are sunk in deep slumber, cheated of such grace!"

Now since the grace and virtue of the Fathers have made me digress to that story, I think I ought to include in this volume that memorable work of charity which I received through the kindness of that great man Archebius; pure chastity, added to a work of charity, is the more noteworthy if it be marked by a variety of beauty, and so the effort of fasting is seen to be pleasing to God when it results in these charitable works.

Chapter 36 - A description of the Diolcian desert, where the hermits dwell. During our training we moved from the monasteries of Palestine to the town in Egypt called Diolcos, and found there, to our admiration, a large number of monks under strict discipline living in the best and earliest form of monasticism. We were encouraged by general advice to make haste to examine and discern the other type of monasticism, which is considered more excellent, that is the life of hermits. These hermits first lived for a long time in monasteries, and were carefully trained in the whole discipline of endurance and discernment. Once possessed of the virtues of humility and poverty, and fully cleansed from all vice, they set off for the unknown recesses of the desert to engage the fiend in fierce conflict. We found men of this description living near the mouth of the Nile, in an island surrounded on one side by the said river, and on the other by the open sea. It was uninhabitable except by monks searching for privacy, for the ground was so salty, and the sands so barren that it was unfit for any cultivation. As I said, we eagerly journeyed to see them, and were exceedingly impressed by their efforts, which they endured in the quest for virtue and love of solitude. For they were so restricted by lack even of water that they distributed it with more scrupulous care than even the most careful butler would use in keeping or serving the finest wine. They brought water for their needs three miles or more from a branch of the River, a distance they had to cover twice with extreme difficulty across the sand dunes that intervened.

Chapter 37 - What Abba Archebius said to us, and how he built cells.
When we had seen them, and were inspired by the desire of imitating them, Archebius, whom I have mentioned before, most esteemed among them for his kindness, invited us to his cell. Once he had discovered how interested we were, he pretended that he wanted to leave that place, and offered his cell to us as if he were moving away, asserting that he would have done so anyway even if we had not arrived. This fired us with the desire to stay, and, trusting such a man's statement unquestioningly, we gladly took him at his word and accepted his cell with all its furnishing and utensils. And so, using a holy equivocation, he left the region for a few days, long enough to get together the materials to construct a cell, and coming back afterwards, built himself another with great effort. Not long after some more brothers arrived, with the same desire of dwelling there, and with the same charitable pretence he again abandoned his cell to them with all its fittings. He himself, unwearied in the work of charity, built himself a third cell, and there he remained.

Chapter 38 - How the same Archebius paid off his mother's debts by his own labour.

It seems worthwhile for me to tell of another work of charity by the same man, so that the monks of our country may be inspired by an example, in the same person, not only of strict self-control, but also of genuine love and affection. For he was born in a considerable family, but leaving this world and his parents' love, he fled as a youth to the monastery, which was about four miles from the town I have mentioned. Here he spent his whole life in such a way that for fifty years he never again entered the village which he had left, nor did he look at the face of any woman, not even his mother. But then his father died, leaving debts of a hundred shillings. Although he himself was totally free from any anxiety, being quite alienated from his family affairs, he discovered that his mother was being pressed by the creditors. Then he, having followed the Gospel advice to call no man on earth his father or mother while his parents were still living in prosperity, was moved by filial love to acknowledge his mother, and made haste to help her in her distress, though relaxing none of his usual restraints. For he remained within the monastic enclosure, and determined to triple the output of his usual work. Thus slaving by day and night for a whole year, by his own toil he paid the due sum to the creditors, and set his mother free from all worry. He lifted the burden of the debt from her, but allowed nothing of his strict way of life to be diminished while performing this devoted and necessary work. He kept his usual seclusion, in no way denying the work of love for his mother's distress, for he acknowledged again out of filial duty the mother he had previously deserted for the love of Christ.

Chapter 39 - How one of the elders craftily provided work for Abba Symeon when he was unemployed.

When our dearest brother Symeon arrived from Italy, being quite ignorant of Greek, one of the elders who wanted to be charitable towards this stranger under cover of employing him, asked why he sat idle in his cell, adding that he could not remain thus for long, both through the danger of idleness and lack of necessary sustenance; moreover that no one could long endure the loneliness unless he were content to earn his own living with his own hands. He answered that he could do nothing, and was unskilled in all the things which the brothers did there, but could write like a scribe if anyone in that part of Egypt had any use for a Latin book. The other, seizing the opportunity to offer a work of charity under cover of paying a wage, said "This is a God-sent chance! I had been long looking for someone to copy St Paul for me in Latin; for I have a brother in the army who knows Latin well, and I want to send him something of the Scriptures to read and to edify him." Symeon gladly took the opportunity as one sent him by God, and the elder freely kept up the pretence which gave him a chance to perform a work of mercy generously; he brought him immediately all he would need for a whole year calling them his wages, and he even brought parchment and the necessary equipment for writing, till he received his book, which was of no use or profit at all, (for this language is totally unknown to everyone in that region), except that he profited by this clever generosity. Thus the one earned his living through his own skill and labour, without any shame or embarrassment, and the other performed his act of charity as if it were a just remuneration, gaining for himself all the more reward that in his affection for the stranger monk he not only provided the necessities of life but also the tools of his work and an occasion to use them.

Chapter 40 - Of how some boys who were taking figs to a sick monk died of hunger in the desert without eating them.

Now we were supposed to be speaking of fasting and abstinence in this book, but works of affection and charity seem to have intruded, so let us return to our subject, and insert into this book a memorable story of some who were youthful in years, but not in sense. Someone brought some figs from the Mareotic district of Libya (and they surpass all estimation) to Abba John, the bursar in the Scythian desert, as something never before seen in that region, for in the days of the blessed priest Paphnutius he had been put in charge of supplies for the church. Abba John immediately sent them on, in charge of two youths, to an old man who was gravely ill in the remoter part of the desert, eighteen miles away from the church. The boys took the fruit and headed for the old monk's cell, which even the older ones could normally reach easily, but as a thick fog suddenly descended, they lost their way. They wandered all day and all night through the trackless waste, and could not find the sick monk's cell; at length they sank to their knees, through weariness of the journey, hunger and thirst, and rendered their souls to the Lord while they were at prayer. They were found much later by following their footprints, which in those sandy parts can be as clearly impressed as in snow, until the light sand, stirred by the slightest breeze, cover them again; and the figs were found untouched, preserved as they had received them, for they had preferred to lay down their lives rather than betray their trust, better to lose their life in this world than to disobey the orders of their superior.

Chapter 41 - The teaching of Abba Macarius, of how a monk should live as if he were to live for ever, or as if he were to die every day.
The blessed Macarius leaves us a salutary piece of teaching, to close this volume on fasting and self-control with such a great man's words. "A monk," he said, "should give himself to fasting as if he were to live a hundred years in this body; he should restrain the wandering mind and forget wrongs, reject melancholy and think nothing of grief and suffering, as if he were to die this day." In the former lies useful and wise discernment, which leads a monk to proceed always with a reasonable regime, and not to allow bodily weakness to turn him away from austerity to dangerous extremes; by the latter comes greatness of heart, leading to salvation, which learns not only to spurn the seeming prosperity of this world, but also not to be crushed by tragedy and to treat disasters as of no importance, keeping the mind constantly fixed on heaven, whither day by day he might believe himself to be on the point of passing.

BOOK SIX

Of the Spirit of Fornication

Chapter 1 - On the twofold struggle against the Spirit of Fornication.

Our second round, as the Fathers have taught us, is the fight against the spirit of fornication, which takes longer than the others; an endless epic battle, which few win completely. Human nature begins to fight it from the moment of puberty, and the war is not over until all the other vices have been overthrown. Now this enemy is twofold, armed for the battle with twin vices, so that it must be resisted with a twofold shield. Since it gains its strength from a disease of mind and body together, it cannot be conquered except by fighting on both fronts. Bodily fasting alone is not enough to win and acquire pure and perfect chastity, unless we prepare for it with a contrite heart, and with persistent prayer against this foul fiend, accompanied by regular meditation on Scripture. We need in addition spiritual wisdom, and strenuous manual labour which concentrates and directs the wandering thoughts, and above all a properly grounded real humility, without which no victory can ever be won against any vice at all.

Chapter 2 - Of the principal remedy against fornication.

The antidote to this vice is found mainly in perfection of heart, for it is the heart, as Our Lord tells us, from which the virus of this disease emanates. "From the heart," he says, "emerge evil thoughts, murder, adultery, fornication, theft and false witness." (*Matth. 15:19*) The heart is, therefore that we must first control, for we know to be the fountain both of life and of death; as Solomon says, "Guard your heart with all diligence, for thence is the spring of life." (*Prov. 4:23, LXX*) The flesh follows its decision and command, and therefore fasting and abstinence are to be diligently practised, lest the flesh be crammed with too much food, come into conflict with the healthy urges of the soul, and, growing haughty, repudiate the spirit which is its master. However, if we put all our effort into chastising the body, while the soul does not fast in a similar way from other vices, and is not busied in prayerful meditation and spiritual reading, we cannot hope to rise to the airy heights of true integrity, while our higher faculties still jeopardise the purity of the body. As Our Lord says, we should "first cleanse the inside of cup and dish, so that the outside may be clean as well." (*Matth. 23:26*)

Chapter 3 - How much solitude and self-control contribute to overcoming sexual vice.
Other vices are usually cleansed by contact with other people in daily life, and are to some degree cured by the shame of the lapse itself; for instance the failings of wrath, melancholy and impatience are healed by interior meditation, watchful care, and the company of the brethren with their constant example. Hence the more often these vices are displayed, and the more strenuously they are contradicted, the quicker they are healed. This vice, on the other hand, as well as bodily penance and heartfelt sorrow, needs also solitary isolation, so that a state of integrity may result, putting aside the dangerous heats of passion. It is often beneficial for those suffering from certain diseases not even to allow them to set eyes on dangerous foods, lest a deadly desire arise simply by looking at them; in the same way quiet and solitude contribute much to dispel this particular disease, for the sick mind is not confronted with a variety of people, and thus may arrive at a more pure inner sight, and may more easily eradicate the infectious germ of lust.

Chapter 4 - The difference between self-restraint and chastity, and whether both may be held together.
No one should suppose that I am denying that self-restrained men may be found even in a community of monks, and in fact we acknowledge this to be very likely. But it is one thing to be continent, that is self-restrained, and another thing to be chaste, which is the progression to a longing for that undefiled integrity, which is called purity. This virtue in its fullness is only attributed to those who remain

virginal both in body and mind, such as the two Johns we meet in the New Testament, and Elias, Jeremias and Daniel in the Old. In this state those too are rightly counted who, having experienced a fall, attain to a similar state of purity through long effort and careful restraint of mind and body. They may feel the urges of the flesh, but simply as a natural occurrence rather than as the assaults of base desire. I believe that it is very difficult to achieve this state among a crowd of people; whether it be really impossible let no one expect to discover from me, but search in his own conscience. However there is no doubt that there are many self-restrained men who can resist and overcome the urges of the flesh, whether they experience them rarely or every day, either through fear of Hell or love of the Kingdom of Heaven. The elders consider that such men, granted that they cannot be entirely overwhelmed by temptations to sin, yet can never be off-guard as if they were invulnerable. For it must happen that one who is in the thick of battle, however often he may repel and overthrow the foe, finds himself scratched at least to some extent.

Chapter 5 - That the sexual urges cannot be overcome by human effort alone.
Therefore, if we long to engage legitimately in the spiritual conflict, with St Paul, *(II Tim. 4:7)* and to overcome the foul fiend wholeheartedly, we should be eager for it, not trusting in our own strength (for human effort is unable to achieve this) but in God's aid. It is necessary for the soul to endure the attacks of this vice until we acknowledge that we are fighting a war beyond our strength, and that we are unable to gain the victory by our own effort and determination, unless we be supported by the help and protection of Our Lord.

Chapter 6 - Of the special grace of God needed for attaining chastity.
Now since in every advance in virtue, and every victory over vice, the grace and the glory are the Lord's, so in this case in particular, those who deserve to attain it must recognise it as a special gift granted by God, as is clearly seen both in what the Fathers have taught and in our experience during this purification. Indeed it is like departing from the

flesh while still in the body; it is beyond nature, for those enveloped in frail flesh, not to feel its urges. It is not possible for a man to soar on his own wings, so to speak, to such an exalted and heavenly height, unless the grace of God lift him from the mud of earth by the virtue of chastity. There is no other virtue which so well equates mortal men with the angelic spirits, in imitation of their manner of life, as the meritorious grace of chastity through which, while still dwelling on earth, we may have citizenship of heaven, as the Apostle puts it. (*Phil. 3:20*) This is to enjoy, while still in the frailty of the body, the dwelling-place promised to the saints to come once they have laid down the burden of flesh. (*Matth. 22:30*)

Chapter 7 - An example taken from worldly games, in the Apostle's words.
Hear what St Paul says: "All who compete in the Games are very abstemious." (*I Cor. 9:25*) Abstemious from what, we ask - so that by comparison with physical games we may learn something about the spiritual conflict. For those who attempt to compete legitimately in visible contests are not allowed to eat any sort of food that they might feel tempted by, but may only eat what their trainer permits for their regime. It is not only eating that is restricted, but they have to abstain from drinking to excess, as well as from any sort of idleness, leisure and relaxation, so that their strength may be increased by daily exercise and constant care. Moreover they are banned from worrying about or being concerned with any secular business, or even marital relationships, so that they are busy about nothing but their strict training, and are not implicated in any worldly affairs. They rely for their daily sustenance totally on the President of the Games, from whom also they aspire to receive with praise the crown of glory and the prize that goes with victory. They are so careful to keep themselves clean from any sexual encounter when they are preparing for a great event, that, lest by chance a nocturnal emission caused by a dream diminish the strength they have spent so long acquiring, they cover their loins with lead plates, so that the contact of the cold metal on their genitals may restrain any sexual arousal. They know that they

will certainly be defeated and be no longer able to perform with full strength in the scheduled event, if a fantasy of lust were to corrupt their solidly grounded modesty.

Chapter 8 - Comparison with the purification of those who compete in earthly competitions.
We should understand how earthly sportsmen are trained, for St Paul wished us to learn from their example, and taught us by observing how careful, how persistent and how strict they are, what should we do in order to preserve the purity of our bodies and the chastity of our minds; we who must daily feed on the flesh of the Most Holy Lamb, which even the regulations of the Old Law permitted no one unclean to touch. For in Leviticus it is laid down that "All who are clean shall eat the flesh," and, "The soul in which there is uncleanness, who eats of the flesh of the saving sacrifice which is of the Lord, that soul shall perish before the Lord." (*Lev. 7:19-20 LXX*) How great therefore is the gift of integrity, without which even those who were bound by the Old Law could not take part in their shadowy sacrifices, and those who desire to gain the fading honours of this world cannot attain the crown!

Chapter 9 - What purity of heart we should display in the sight of God.
The secret thoughts of the heart should first be purified with due care. What they attempt to gain by physical continence, we should possess in the depths of conscience. There sits the Lord, as umpire and referee, watching our efforts in race and competition, so that what we would be ashamed to display in public should not be allowed to arise in our unguarded private thoughts, and we be not defiled by consenting secretly to what we would be ashamed to have known by men. We can elude the notice of men, but can never deceive the holy angels and the wisdom of Almighty God, from whom no secrets are hid.

Chapter 10 - The proof of true purity.
The clearest proof of this sort of purity is demonstrated if when we

are in bed and are relaxed in sleep no fantasy occurs, or at least is unable to stir up any feelings of lust. It is true that these feelings are in no way to be considered really sinful, but when fantasies of this sort stir the imagination, it is evidence of a mind that is not yet perfect, an indication that vice has not been totally eradicated.

Chapter 11 - The cause of nocturnal emissions.

The nature of our thoughts, carelessly guarded during the distractions of the day, are shown up during our nightly repose, so that when fantasies of this sort arise the fault should not be considered to do with sleeping, but with carelessness during the preceding time; it demonstrates a deeply rooted morbidity, which is not the product of the first hours of night. It is something concealed in the interior fibres of the soul, which rises to the surface when it is relaxed in sleep, thus giving proof of hidden lustful urgings which we have been storing up all day long while browsing on evil thoughts. In the same way bodily illnesses do not originate at the moment in which they appear, but are acquired through carelessness during the preceding period, when one has fed on foods dangerous to his health and generated harmful and eventually deadly humours.

Chapter 12 - How physical continence cannot be acquired without purity of heart.

God, the creator and founder of the human race, who knows better than anyone the nature of his handiwork and how to improve it, applied the remedy to that part, whence he knew the principal origins of disease to emanate: "Whoever looks at a woman to lust after her, " he says, "has already committed adultery with her in his heart." (*Matth. 5:28*) Observing a roving eye, he blames not so much the eye as the intention of the mind which uses the ability to see so badly. For the heart is sick, bruised by the impact of lust which it sees and desires. The blessing of sight which the Creator granted it for a good purpose is distorted by its own fault to serve evil ends, and through what it sees, it generates the disease of lust secretly within itself. Hence the saving command is given to the heart, whose depravity causes the evil misuse of sight. For it is not said, "Guard your eyes with all diligence", although it would be well to guard them indeed, if it were from them that lust arises, but the eyes do no more than simply give sight to the mind; no, it is said, "Guard your heart with all diligence;" (*Prov. 4:23 LXX*) apply the remedy especially to that part which can be led astray by the work of the eyes.

Chapter 13 - What is the first precaution towards cleansing the flesh?
This is the first precaution to purify the heart: that when the image of a woman creeps into our minds through the subtle insinuation of our enemy, first of all through remembering a mother, sisters, aunts, or indeed female saints, let us be quick to eliminate these memories from our recollection, lest we linger too long over them and the seducer of evil, taking advantage of their sex, may cause our minds to proceed to become obsessed by these persons, so that he can infiltrate evil thoughts through them. Therefore we should always remember the injunction, "Guard your heart with all diligence," and according to God's first command, be watchful for the poisonous head of the serpent, that is the first arising of evil thoughts, by which the devil tries to wriggle into our minds. Nor should we carelessly allow the rest of his body to penetrate our hearts, that is giving consent to the distraction. Be sure that if he is once allowed in, his deadly bite will destroy the conquered mind. For we should "drown the sinners of this world", (*Psalm 100/1:8*) that is we should quash our fleshly feelings as they first arise, and "dash the children of Babylon on the rock", (*Psalm 136/7:9*) while they are yet small. For if they are not destroyed while they are still weak, they will rise up, fully grown, all the stronger to destroy us through our own connivance, and will certainly not be defeated without great effort and labour. For while a strong man (that is, our spirit) "fully armed, guards its own house", fortifying the recesses of its heart through fear of God, "all his substance will be at peace", (*Luke 11:21*) that is to say the fruits of labour, and virtues built up over a long time. But if "a stronger man come and overthrow him", that is if thoughts consent to the devil, "he will shatter the arms he relied on", that is the memory of Scripture and the fear of God,

and "will divide the spoils", that is, through the contrary vices, he will disperse the virtues that had once been earned.

Chapter 14 - That we should not be concerned to praise chastity, but to explain its practise.
To pass over so much that is said in Holy Scripture in praise of this virtue (for it is not my intention to compose an encomium on chastity, but to explain from the teaching of the Fathers what chastity is, how it can be acquired and preserved, and what its purpose is), I will only quote one sentence of St Paul the Apostle, which shows how when he wrote to the Thessalonicans, he extolled that virtue above all others, recommending it with such earnestness:

Chapter 15 - How the Apostle calls chastity in particular the virtue of holiness.
"This", he says, "is the will of God and your sanctification." (*I Thess. 4:3*) And lest we remain in doubt or are uncertain what it is he wants to call sanctification, whether it be justice, charity, humility or patience, through all of which virtues we may believe we can attain sanctification, he continues to specify which he particularly wishes to designate sanctification: "This is the will of God and your sanctification, that you abstain from fornication, that each one of you learn how to preserve your vessels in holiness and dignity, and not in the turmoil of desire as do the pagans who know not God." (*I Thess. 4:3-5*) See how he praises this virtue, naming it as the dignity of our vessels (that is, of our bodies) and our holiness. And in contrast, those in the turmoil of desire are sunk in shameful uncleanness, and far removed from holiness. He mentions it again a little further on, again calling it sanctification." For God did not call us in uncleanness, but in sanctification. So he who despises this despises not a man but the very God who gave us his Holy Spirit." (*ibid. 7-8*) He adds weight to this unchangeable commandment, saying, "He who despises this," that is the virtue of holiness I have just mentioned, "despises not a man," that is myself who tells you this, "but the very God" who speaks through me, who has himself made our hearts a dwelling place for the

Holy Spirit. Observe with what simple straightforward language he proclaims this, and what praise he gives it, firstly attributing holiness to this particular virtue, secondly showing that through this means the vessel of our bodies can be set free from uncleanness, thirdly explaining how shame and disgrace are banished and our hearts may remain in dignity and holiness, and lastly, proclaiming that through this the Holy Spirit will come to dwell in our hearts, which is the peak of perfection and our joyous reward.

Chapter 16 - Another passage of the Apostle about the same virtue of chastity.
Though we are approaching the end of this book, I will add another text of St Paul similar to the foregoing. He writes thus to the Hebrews: "Pursue peace before all men, and holiness, without which no one shall see God." (*Heb. 12:14*) Clearly he is saying that it is impossible to see God without holiness, which he normally defines as integrity of mind and purity of body, since he continues here in the same way, giving the same meaning, "let no one be a fornicator or a worldly man like Esau." (*ibid. 16*)

Chapter 17 - How the hope of reward to come should increase our concern for chastity.
The more exalted and heavenly the reward of chastity, the more it is assaulted by the heaviest attacks of our enemy. Hence we should be greatly concerned not only for bodily continence but also for contrition in the heart, won by faithful prayers and groans, so that the dew of the Holy Spirit may descend into our hearts and quench that fiery furnace of the flesh which the King of Babylon never ceases to kindle with the sparks of carnal thoughts.

Chapter 18 - Chastity depends on humility, and wisdom on chastity.
The elders tell us that we cannot acquire chastity, unless the heart be first well-grounded in humility, and that we cannot attain to the fountain of true wisdom, as long as the root of this vice still lurks in the recesses of our minds. It is possible to attain integrity without the

grace of wisdom, but impossible to acquire divine wisdom without chaste integrity. For there is a variety of gifts, and the grace of the Holy Spirit is not given in the same way to all, but each one is granted that grace for which he had made himself ready and apt by his persistent efforts. And so although we believe that all the Apostles possessed the virtue of perfect chastity, yet the gift of wisdom abounded especially in Paul, since he had made himself ready for it through his own determination.

Chapter 19 - A saying of St Basil, about his virginity.
A saying of Saint Basil, Bishop of Caesarea, is recorded: "I have never known a woman, yet I am not a virgin." By this he means that purity of the flesh does not lie merely in abstinence from women, but in singleness of heart, which is the perpetual guardian of unsullied holiness of the body, either through fear of God or love of chastity.

Chapter 20 - What is the goal of perfect purity of mind.
The culmination and perfect proof of purity, is if while we are asleep no impure thought creep over us, and if nature demands that seed should flow, then it happens while we are unconscious of it. It would be unnatural to be totally without such emissions and be forever free from them, but the peak of virtue is when they occur only very infrequently as nature demands, which usually happens to a monk about once every two months. This I write from my own experience, not as the elders taught, who consider even this period of intermission to be still too little; for I was afraid that if I tried to propound the measure of purity which we learnt from them, I should be credited with describing what is unbelievable or impossible by those who have achieved a lesser degree of purity, either through carelessness or lack of concentration.

Chapter 21 - How we may recover a state of perfect purity.
We can maintain this state continually and never fall short of the natural interval, the time I have mentioned above, if we not only

consider that God observes our secret actions, and even our thoughts, all day and all night, and is conscious of them, but we also acknowledge that it is to him that we must render an account for all that passes in our hearts, as well as our actions and works.

Chapter 22 - To what extent our purity of body may be brought, and what indication there is of purity in mind.

Let us therefore make haste to reach this point, and combat the wandering mind and the urges of the flesh in such a way that our physical nature may perform its natural functions without arousing lust, and seed may be emitted without disturbing us or causing any affront to our chastity. For as long as the mind, though still asleep, is ensnared by a fantasy in dream, it should know that it has still not reached the perfection of true purity

Chapter 23 - The remedy through which perfect chastity of heart and body may be established.

Now to prevent these fantasies from creeping up on us, even in our sleep, we should preserve a steady, moderate and consistent fast. For anyone who exceeds the proper degree of abstinence, will certainly exceed the measure of relaxation as well. If he goes to extremes he will undoubtedly fail to maintain the level of tranquillity. One moment he is weak through too much austerity, the next he is bloated with overeating. If you continually change the pattern of eating, the pattern of your purity is bound to change as well. We must therefore always exercise humility twinned with patience, and a careful vigilance during the daytime against anger and the other vices. For where the poison of wrath enters, the fires of lust will certainly follow. But above all we need to take especial care at night, for as purity and watchfulness by day prepare the way for chastity at night, so nightly prayer anticipates a solid and consistent strength of heart in our daytime care.

BOOK SEVEN

Of the Spirit of Avarice

Chapter 1 - How the war against Avarice takes us out of ourselves, for it is not natural to us as other vices are.

The third round of our fight is against avarice, which we may define as love of money. It is a war against an outside foe, not part of our nature, and it arises in a monk for no other reason than a lazy, corrupt and sluggish mind, when his renunciation of the world has been badly begun, grounded on a love of God that is only lukewarm. The roots of the other vices are integral to human nature, and seem to have genetic origins within ourselves, innate in the flesh; being already there when we are born, they antedate the knowledge of good and evil. Though they are the first to seize on a man, it takes long efforts to overcome them.

Chapter 2 - How dangerous the vice of avarice is.

This disease, on the other hand, arises later, and comes into the mind from outside, and although we may easily guard against it and repel it, yet if we are unwary and once let it into our hearts it proves most dangerous, and very difficult to eliminate. It becomes indeed the root of all evil, *(I Tim. 6:10)* bearing fruit containing the seeds of innumerable vices.

Chapter 3 - The value to us of natural vices.

Consider that the normal arousal of the flesh can be observed not only in children who are still innocent and unable to distinguish good from evil, but even in babies at the breast. They have not even the slightest interest in lust, which shows that the physical arousal occurs from a natural cause. And we can see the same sort of indications of violent anger in children, as they display a reaction to things they dislike; before they can learn the virtue of patience they can detect a verbal rebuke, even if it is in play. They may well not have the ability but they certainly have the will to avenge themselves when they are provoked to anger. I do not mean to imply that we are to blame for this natural condition, but to explain that these reactions which arise from within ourselves may be given to us for a good reason, whereas others enter us from outside, either through laziness or deliberate malice. The physical arousal which I mentioned is for the sake of continuing our inheritance and generating the next generation, and is given to our bodies through the Creator's providence - it is not for abuse, or for adultery, which is condemned by the authority of the law. And we can recognise that the instinct for anger is beneficial to us, so that we may be enraged at our own vices and mistakes and be all the more zealous for virtue and spiritual learning, in order to display our total love of God and kindness towards our brethren. We can find a value in sorrow as well, although when it is turned towards the wrong end it is numbered among the other vices. Fear also is very necessary, when it is directed towards God, though it is pernicious enough when directed at this world - as St Paul tells us, "A sorrow with regard to God causes repentance for eternal salvation, but the sorrow of this world causes death." (II Cor. 7)

Chapter 4 - How we can say that certain vices are natural to us without blaming the Creator.

Now if we say that these emotions were implanted in us by the Creator, it does not imply that he is to blame if we abuse them by wickedly perverting them to evil ends, if we prefer to sorrow over fruitless worldly wealth, rather than over repentance for salvation and the elimination of vice, or indeed if we feel anger not against ourselves and profitably, but against our brethren contrary to our Lord's command. Suppose you were to be given an axe for some necessary use, and preferred to abuse it by killing the innocent, you could not blame the smith who made it, if you were to use for murder what he provided for uses both necessary and beneficial to life.

Chapter 5 - On vices which are acquired through our own fault without any natural instinct.

There are certain vices which arise without any preceding natural cause, but simply from a corrupt and deliberate malice, vices such as envy, and our present subject, avarice. These do not originate in us by natural instinct, but are acquired from without. They may be easy to avoid, and readily rejected, but if they gain a hold over the mind, they render it miserable, and scarcely allow it any remedy to restore it to health. This is either because those who are wounded by this vice do not deserve to be cured by a swift-acting medicine, for they could easily have ignored, avoided or conquered it, or because they are too badly formed to be fit to attain the whole of virtue and the pinnacle of perfection.

Chapter 6 - How difficult it is to expel the disease of avarice once contracted.

No one should underestimate or despise this problem, since although it can be easily avoided, yet if it gain a hold on anyone it is scarcely possible to bring it to a satisfactory cure. It is indeed a very sink of vice, the root of all evils, and produces the germs of incurable wickedness. As St Paul says, "The love of money", that is, avarice, "is the root of all evil." (*I Tim. 6:10*)

Chapter 7 - The vices which breed avarice, and how many evils it breeds in turn.

When this vice first fastens on a slack or lazy monk, it begins by worrying him about little amounts, under quite reasonable pretexts, on the grounds of which it suggests he ought to keep by or acquire a little money. It points out that what the monastery provides is not enough, and quite inadequate for a healthy strong body. How could he cope if his physical health were to break down, and no special fund had been set aside to treat the illness? The monastic fare is very meagre, and the care of the sick quite inadequate. If he had nothing of his own to attend to his physical needs, he would be bound to die in misery. For that matter the clothing provided is insufficient, and he must find something else to supplement it. Nor can he remain too long in one place or one monastery, and unless he saves up his travel expenses and his fare for a sea-crossing, he would be unable to move when he wanted to, and would be forced by sheer poverty to put up with a tedious wretched life without any advancement. He would be always needy and bare, and indeed reproached for living off another's bounty. With thoughts like these it entangles the mind, till he decides how to acquire just one denarius. Then he diligently pursues his own private work, without the abbot's knowledge, sells what he has made, and at last is in possession of the desired sum. But then he becomes worried and anxious how to double it, unsure where to keep it, or to whom to entrust it. Then he is even more worried about what to invest it in, and what sort of trade would double it. When this desire has been quietened by fulfilment, a greater greed for gold arises, and rages all the more fiercely as the sum deposited becomes greater. The madness of avarice increases with the increase of wealth. Then he promises himself a long life, and a green old age - but that would bring various infirmities which he could not endure unless he made preparations in youth by laying up great savings. Thus the unhappy man is constricted in the serpent's coils, as he longs to increase the wealth he has wrongly amassed by even greater wrongs, bringing to birth a plague which will inflame him worse, wrapt up wholly in the thought of gain, till he has no other concern in mind than how he may acquire money, the quicker to escape from the monastic rule, but with no confidence of achieving any hope of profit. To this end he recoils from no crime, neither deceit, nor perjury, nor theft, not ashamed if he breaks faith, nor if he be overtaken by the evil passion of anger. If he fails in his hope of gain, he is not afraid to exceed the measure of honesty and humility, and just as others make their stomachs into gods, so he does gold and profit. The holy Apostle, considering the poisonous nature of this disease, not only calls it the root of all evil, but even the service of idols, when he says, "and avarice," (which is *philargyria* in Greek), "which is servitude to idols." (*Col. 3:5*) You see how this madness grows little by little to an utter downfall, till St Paul can call it servitude to idols or false gods, since the image and likeness of God is lost (which a devout servant of God should preserve without stain in himself), and he prefers to love and contemplate gold stamped with the image of a man, rather than God.

Chapter 8 - How avarice impedes all other virtues.
As he grows worse by these gradual stages, he is discontented, retaining not even the shadow, let alone the virtue of humility, of charity, or of obedience, being wrathful at everything, and complaining and sighing over every action. With no remaining reverence, he rushes headlong over the cliff, like a runaway horse unchecked; content neither with his daily fare nor the usual clothing, and affirms he cannot tolerate it any longer. He asserts that God is not to be found in the monastery, nor can he assure his salvation enclosed in that one place. Hence he complains that if he does not take himself off as soon as possible, he will be bound to perish.

Chapter 9 - That a monk who possesses money cannot persevere in the community.
Now once he is unstable, and in possession of the travel expenses, he relies on them to make himself wings, as it were, and being ready to leave, gives an insolent answer to every command. He behaves like a visitor or outsider, and ignores and disparages any necessary correction he receives. Although he owns a secret horde of money, he complains that he has no shoes or clothing, and is indignant if they are supplied too slowly. And if anything like this is distributed for the use of a senior monk, before him, who is known to have nothing, he fires up with greater anger, considering himself to be undervalued, as if he were an outsider, and is not happy about applying his hand to any work, complaining about everything which the needs of the monastery require. He then looks out for occasions to take offence or become angry, not wanting to appear to leave the monastery for a trivial reason. He is not content just to leave the community, for he might be thought to have deserted through his own fault, but ceaselessly denigrates it in private conversations. And if he is unable to depart through bad weather affecting roads or sea-crossings, he

remains for the whole time anxious and disturbed, never ceasing to brood over his woes and vent them, till he finds relief in departing, an excuse for his fickleness, and something to blame in the monastery, not in himself.

Chapter 10 - How a deserter from the monastery, who had been grumbling under the lightest inconvenience, undergoes great labours for the sake of money.
As the flames of avarice are enkindled more and more and take possession of him, they do not permit the monk to remain in the monastery, nor to live under the discipline of a rule. Like a wild beast separating a sheep from the flock to become its prey, avarice deprives him of his companions, and removes him from the community home the easier to devour him. Then he who began by finding the light work of the monastery distasteful, is forced to toil untiringly day and night in the hope of profit; he is not permitted to celebrate the office, nor to keep the rule of fasting, nor the customary vigils; he cannot fulfil the obligations of charitable intercession, driven by the need to satisfy this mad avarice, or at least to come by his daily sustenance, for though he imagines that he is extinguishing the fire of avarice by satisfying it, he is in fact fuelling it.

Chapter 11 - How it becomes necessary to employ women for the sake of guarding the money.
Many who have fallen off the precipice so suddenly in this way are unable to check their course and are dashed to their death; they are not content with the mere possession of the property which they had never had before, or had but carelessly saved, but look out for female domestics to take on the task of looking after what was badly arranged and stored. How they entangle themselves with dangerous and dubious business practices, till they fall into the depths of hell! They spurn the Apostle's advice, to "be content with having food and clothing," (*I Tim. 6:8*) which the simple fare of the monastery gave them, but "desiring to become rich they fall into the devil's tempting snares, grasping after many useless or dangerous things which submerge a

man to his utter destruction. The root of all evils is the love of money, that is avarice; in the desire for this many have strayed from the faith and entangled themselves in manifold woes." (*I Tim. 6:9-10*)

Chapter 12 - The example of a certain lax monk, entangled in the snare of avarice.

I was acquainted with one who made himself a monk, and (what is worse) preened himself on his perfection. He was welcomed into a monastery and was admonished by his abbot not to return to the property he had renounced, and to liberate himself from avarice, the root of all evil, and from the snares of this world; moreover if he wished to be cleansed from his basic passions, which seemed to be weighing heavily on him all the time, he should cease to long for things which he had never even possessed before, for there would certainly be no possibility of him succeeding in cleansing himself from vice as long as he was enthralled by such things. But he made no hesitation in replying, with a scowl, "If you have enough property to support so many, why do you prevent me from having as much?"

Chapter 13 - How the elders can help the younger to rid themselves of vice.

No one should consider this advice useless or harmful, for unless the nature of a wound is first probed, and the first causes of a disease diagnosed, it is impossible to apply the appropriate remedy to the sufferer, nor to take proper precautions to preserve the health of the strong. So this advice and much more is usually given in spiritual conferences to the young monks by their elders, who have witnessed so many falling into difficulties. Once we had recognised many of these things in ourselves, as the elders instructed us and informed us, and acknowledged that they too suffered from the same passions, we were cured without the shame of having fallen, through quietly learning both the remedies and the causes of the vices that beset us. Some of these matters we pass over in silence out of respect for the brotherhood, for should this book happen to fall into the hands of those who are less informed about these matters, it would reveal to their ignorance things which should only be learnt by those who have worked hard and fast at attaining the peak of perfection.

Chapter 14 - Examples showing the threefold nature of Avarice.
This disease has three aspects, which the Fathers agree in condemning with equal detestation. The first is that which we have described above, when avarice deceives the wretches and persuades them to hoard up things which they had not possessed even in their former life in the world. The next is when it drives them to claim back and once again require the things which they had cast off at their first renunciation of the world. The third is when they have made a bad and insincere start to monastic life, beginning in imperfection, so that it does not allow those whom it has once infected with this laxity of mind to rid themselves of all their earthly possessions, through fear of poverty and lack of confidence; as a result they keep back those material possessions which they ought to have cast off and repudiated, so that avarice never allows them to attain evangelical perfection. We can find examples of these three types of fall in Holy Scripture, and they are punished with no light penalty. Giezi wanted to acquire things which he had never had before, and thus not only failed to merit the grace of prophecy, which he should have received as a sort of inheritance from his master, but on the contrary was afflicted with a life-long leprosy at the curse of the holy Elishah. (*II Kings 5:27*) Judas, wishing to claim back the money which he had formerly renounced when he followed Christ, did not only fall so low as to betray his Master and lose his rank of apostle, but did not even merit to end his life in a normal manner, but ended it by a double death. (*Matth.27:5*) Ananaias and Sapphira, who kept back part of what they had possessed, were punished with death at the Apostle's word. (*Acts 5:5 and 10*)

Chapter 15 - How a bad monk differs from one who does not renounce the world at all.
Of those who claim to have renounced this world, but are broken by lack of faith and terrified to be stripped of their worldly wealth, there

is a prophetic command in Deuteronomy: "If there be any man timid and fearful of heart", he should not go out to war but, "let him return and go back to his home, lest he cause his brothers' hearts to fear in the manner in which he is fearful and afraid." (*Deut. 20:8*) Now what can be clearer than that? Is it not the evident wish of Scripture that they should not even begin to attempt this way of life, nor to take on the title of monk, rather than call back others from their Evangelical perfection, and weaken them with faithless fear through their bad example and discouragement? They are therefore commanded to draw back from the battle and return home, for no one can fight in the wars of the Lord with a divided heart. "For a man of divided heart is unreliable in all he does." (*James 1:8*) As in that Gospel parable, they should consider whether he who advances to war with ten thousand be unable to resist a king who advances with twenty thousand, but rather should sue for peace while he is still afar off. (*Luke 14:31-2*) That is to say, that they should not take on the monastic life at all, rather than attempt it carelessly and bring a greater rebuke upon themselves. "For it is better not to vow at all, than to vow and not fulfil." (*Eccles. 5:4, LXX*) It is an apt parable, this of the one man with ten thousand and the other with twenty, for the number of vices that war against us is greater than that of virtues which fight on our side. "No man can serve God and Mammon." (*Matth. 6:24*) "Nor can one who puts his hand to the plough, and looks back, be fit for the Kingdom of God." (*Luke 9:62*)

Chapter 16 - How those who are reluctant to dispose of their property find an excuse in Scripture.

There are those who attempt to find authority in Holy Scripture for allowing avarice to take possession of them, for they interpret it with a perverse mind and corrupt the teaching of the Apostle and of our Lord himself, distorting it to match their own desires; they do not adapt their life or opinions to the sense of Scripture, but turn Scripture to serve their own lustful desires. Wishing the text to agree with their opinions, they say that it is written, "It is more blessed to give than to receive." (*Acts 20:35*) By wickedly misinterpreting this, they make the Lord's own teaching void, where He says, "If you wish to be perfect, go, sell all you have and give to the poor, and you will have treasure in heaven, and then come, follow me." (*Matth. 19:21*) Their excuse for not ridding themselves of their riches is that they consider themselves more blessed if they are well endowed with property so that they can give to others out of their own superfluity. Since they are ashamed to be like St Paul, gloriously stripped of everything for the sake of Christ, they are not prepared to be content with the work of their own hands and the fare offered by the monastery. Their choice is, either to acknowledge themselves to be so encumbered that they never renounce the world, and sleep soundly on their inherited wealth; or to desire in very truth to make their monastic profession, and so distribute everything and rid themselves of it, keeping back nothing of what they are giving up, being glad to join the Apostle in "hunger and thirst, in cold and nakedness." (*II Cor. 11:27*)

Chapter 17 - How the Apostles and the early Christians gave up their property.
Surely St Paul, who admits to have been of noble birth by the standards of this world, when he claims that he was dignified from birth with Roman citizenship, (*Acts 22:28*) could have been supported on his own patrimony, had he thought it appropriate on his path to perfection. Those too in Jerusalem, who were possessors of fields or houses and sold everything, keeping nothing at all back for themselves, and brought the value and laid it at the feet of the disciples, (*Acts 4:34-5*) could have supported their earthly needs by their own property, had the apostles considered this the better path, or they themselves had judged it more expedient. But no, they renounced everything they had and preferred to live by their own labour or the collection taken from overseas. St Paul writes to the Romans about this fund, announcing his own role in it, and gently encouraging them to give to the collection, when he says, "Now I am going to Jerusalem to administer to the saints. Macedonia and Greece were pleased to take a collection for the needs of the saints who are in Jerusalem, pleased to be their

debtors in this." (*Romans 15:25-7*) For as the pagans had benefited from their spiritual wealth, so they rightly served them in material things. He brings the same considerations before the Corinthians and warns them to be diligent in taking the collection before he arrives so that he can arrange to send it for the needs of the poor in Jerusalem. "Concerning the collection for the saints, as I had arranged in the church of Galatia, so you should do. Let each one of you put something aside every Sunday, saving as much as you think fit, so that the collection will not need to be taken when I arrive. When I do come, I will send the men you recommended in your letter to take it to Jerusalem and to convey your thanks to them." (*I Cor. 16:1-3*) Then to encourage them to make the collection larger, he adds, "If it is worth while, they can travel with me when I go." That is, if your offering is sufficient to warrant me in accompanying it. Writing to the Galatians, he shows that he had arranged this with James, Peter and John, since he shared the work of preaching with the apostles; although it was his task to preach to the pagans, he was never to forget to be concerned for the poor who were in Jerusalem, those who had given up everything they had for Christ's sake and had brought poverty upon themselves. (*Gal. 2:9-10*) "When they saw the grace of God which was given to me, James and Kephas and John, those seeming pillars of the Church, gave me and Barnabas the hand of friendship, so that we should preach to the pagans, and they to the circumcised, but that we should be mindful of their poor." He shows that he has fulfilled this request diligently saying, "And I was eager to perform this work myself." (*Gal. 2-10*)

So who are the more blessed - those who have recently become converts from paganism, and are unable to attain to evangelical perfection, still relying on their own wealth, in which the Apostle promises them great rewards, since they have turned away from "the worship of idols, from fornication, strangled meat and blood", (*Acts 15:20*) and accepted the faith of Christ with all their property; or those who take up the challenge of the Gospel and carry the Cross of the Lord daily, (*Matth. 10:9*) wishing nothing of their own property to survive? Even St Paul, when he was confined and chained in prison, or was burdened by troublesome journeys, was accustomed to accept his living costs, which he could not earn himself, from the brethren who came from Macedonia as an addition to his income: he acknowledges this debt when he says, "the brothers who came from Macedonia made up what I was lacking." (*II Cor. 11:9*) He also mentions this to the Philippians, "You know well, my Philippians, how when the Gospel was first preached and I departed from Macedonia, there was no church that kept in touch and gave me what I needed except you alone, for once or twice you sent money to me in Thessalonica." (*Phil. 4:15-16*) Can we say, as those others would have it, dim as they are, that the Macedonians were more blessed than the Apostle, because they had enough property to be able to give him something? No one would be so foolish as to claim that!

Chapter 18 - How if we would imitate the Apostles we should not live on our own income but do as they did.

Now if we would obey the Evangelical counsel, and live in imitation of the Apostle Paul and the whole primitive Church, not to mention the Fathers who have inherited their virtues and perfection in our own age, let us not rest on our unearned income, promising ourselves an Evangelical perfection in such a slack and wretched condition, but let us follow in their footsteps and have no worries about our own affairs. Let us pursue the monastic rule and way of life in such a way that we may truly renounce this world, not wavering through lack of faith, and keeping back nothing of what we had given up. Let us win our daily bread by the labour of our own hands, not by inherited wealth.

Chapter 19 - The teaching of St Basil against a Senator.

A saying is preserved of St Basil, Bishop of Caesarea, in contradiction to a certain senator, who was so affected by the slackness we have been describing, that when he claimed to have renounced this world he kept back some of his own property, being unwilling to live by the work of his own hands and to acquire true humility in nakedness and manual labour, following the discipline of the monastery: "You have ruined a senator and failed to produce a monk." (*Here we follow Gazet's text; Petschenig treats the Greek word for senator as a proper name, Syncleticus.*)

Chapter 20 - How shameful it is to be vanquished by avarice.

If we desire to compete legitimately in the spiritual contest, we must expel this dangerous enemy from our hearts. Although it is not very creditable to overcome it, yet it is quite disgraceful to be overcome by it. To be crushed by a strong foe, however much grief there be in subjection, and lamentation for lost triumph, nevertheless brings a certain consolation to the conquered because of the enemy's strength. But if the enemy is weak, and the struggle feeble, besides the grief in being overthrown there is a greater shame and disgrace in falling like this.

Chapter 21 - How avarice may be defeated.

This is what total victory and lasting triumph means, when as it is said, a monk's conscience is untainted by even the slightest sum of money. For it is impossible for one who is defeated in small matters and allows the root of desire to enter his heart, not to be straightway afire with longing for some greater acquisition. A soldier of Christ will be confidently victorious, and unaffected by any attack of desire, as long as this most pernicious spirit fails to sow the seeds of concupiscence in his heart. Therefore while we must be on our guard in general against the serpent's head with regard to all types of vice, in this case in particular we must be especially careful. If it once be admitted, it will grow on its own substance and enkindle fiercer flames of its own accord. We must not only beware the possession of money, but even root out the very desire of it from our minds. The effect of avarice is not to be shunned as much as the affection for it is to be eradicated. It would be useless to be without money is we retained the intention of possessing it.

Chapter 22 - How one can be convicted of avarice even without possessing money.

It is possible for someone who owns no money to be still in no way free from avarice, and for poverty to be of no use to him at all, if he has been unable to eliminate the vice of desire, and chooses poverty for its own sake, not for the sake of virtue, content with simplicity but not without heartfelt yearnings. Just as the Gospel can accuse men of adultery even if they have not physically committed it, (*Matth. 5:28*) so those who are scarcely affected by the burden of riches may be guilty of avarice in mind and desire. They wanted only the occasion, not the free will, which is what God always rewards more than compulsion. Let us be quick, therefore, not to lose the benefit of our labour for nothing. It would be wretched to endure poverty and want, and then to lose the benefit of it through our own weak will.

Chapter 23 - The example of Judas.
Do you want to understand what a dangerous and evil fruit this seed may bear, if it be not carefully eliminated, to the destruction of its host, branching out into vices of all kinds? Look at Judas, ranked among the Apostles, who was not prepared to crush the deadly head of this serpent. See how its poison corrupted him, and the coils of desire encircled him, driving him to so terrible an offence, that it persuaded him to sell the Redeemer of the World, the Saviour of humankind, for thirty pieces of silver. He would never have been lured to so shameful a betrayal had he not been corrupted by the evil of avarice. He would never have been guilty of the blasphemous death of the Lord, had he not first become accustomed to plundering the purse entrusted to him.

Chapter 24 - How avarice cannot be overcome except by poverty.
That is a clear example of this terrible tyranny which, once it has ensnared the mind, as we have seen, allows us to maintain no standard of honour, and is never satisfied however much we may acquire. This madness can be stayed only by poverty, not by riches. Judas was entrusted with the funds intended for the relief of the poor, and embezzled them in order to put an end to his desire for money by having abundance of wealth, but the more he acquired the more the

seed of desire grew, till he was not content just with secretly plundering the funds, but went on to sell the Lord Himself. The folly of avarice exceeds the greatest possible riches.

Chapter 25 - On the deaths of Ananias and Sapphira, and of Judas, brought on them by the lust for riches.

The Prince of the Apostles, warned by this example, knew that nothing can bridle those who are gripped by avarice, and neither small nor great wealth can satisfy it but only real poverty. He punished Ananias and Sapphira (whom we mentioned above) with death, because they kept back part of their property, so that they might receive as the reward of their cupidity the death which Judas brought on himself through guilt at the Lord's betrayal. (*Acts 5*) How similar the crime, how similar the punishment! In one case avarice led to betrayal, in the other to deceit. One betrayed the Truth, the others sank to the guilt of a lie. Different though the results of their crimes were, the same end came upon them all. Judas recoiled from poverty and tried to recover what he had renounced; Ananias and Sapphira, through fear of poverty, tried to keep back something of their property which they should have faithfully handed over to the Apostles or distributed totally to the brethren. The punishment of death overtook them in both cases, since both crimes sprang from the root of avarice. If in the one case they did not covet other peoples' wealth but tried to retain their own, not desiring to accumulate but only to preserve, yet so severe a condemnation befell them; what shall we think of those who long to acquire money which they have never owned, and while professing poverty before men, are shown up to be rich in God's eyes through their desire for money?

Chapter 26 - How avarice brings a spiritual leprosy on the soul.

From the example of Giezi (*II Kings 5:27*) who lusted for the fading riches of this world and was punished with the infection of unclean leprosy, we can recognise the leprous in mind and spirit. He was a warning to us of how every soul that is tainted with desire becomes infected with the leprosy of vice, and is counted as unclean and accursed forever before the Lord.

Chapter 27 - Texts from Scripture to show how one who desires perfection must not take back what he has once renounced.

Now if you have given up all things for the sake of perfection, following Christ who says to you, "Go, sell all you have and give to the poor, and you will have treasure in heaven, then come, follow me" (*Matth. 19:21*) why do you look back after your hand is set to the plough, as the Lord also says, (*Luke 9:62*) calling you unfit for the Kingdom of Heaven? If you are safe on the rooftop of the Gospel, why go down to collect something from your house, something of what you had already rejected? Once at work in the field of virtue, why run back to clothe yourself again in the trappings of this world which you had cast off and abandoned? (*Luke 17:31*) And if your preceding poverty meant that you had nothing to renounce, how much less should you be longing to acquire property which you had never possessed? The Lord has prepared His blessings in this way, so that you may run more quickly towards Him if you are unencumbered by clinging wealth. And indeed no one is too poor to benefit, for everyone has something to give up. Anyone who has radically cut off the desire of possessing it has made the renunciation of all the wealth of the world.

Chapter 28 - How the victory over avarice cannot be gained save through poverty.

How to gain a complete victory over avarice is not to allow the slightest amount of smouldering material to remain in our hearts, for be sure that we will never be able to extinguish it if we cherish even the least tinder for this spark.

Chapter 29 - How a monk may preserve his poverty.

We will never be able to preserve this virtue unstained unless we remain in the monastery, content, as St Paul says, with what we eat and what we wear. (*II Tim 6:8*)

Chapter 30 - Remedies for the plague of avarice.
Keep in mind the condemnation of Ananias and Sapphira, and shun any reservation of what we have pledged ourselves to renounce. Tremble too at the example of Giezi who was afflicted with permanent leprosy in punishment for avarice, and beware of acquiring things which we did not possess before. Fearful too of the reward and the death of Judas, avoid absolutely any taking back of money which you have once rejected. As well as all this, remember how frail and uncertain our life is, and beware lest the day of the Lord come upon us "like a thief in the night", (I Thess. 5:4) and find your soul stained even by a halfpenny. That would be enough to deprive us of all the benefit of our renunciation, and would bring upon us the Lord's sentence, as pronounced over the rich man in the Gospel - "Thou fool: this very night they require thy soul of thee, and whose then shall be the riches thou hast hoarded?" (*Luke 12:20*) Thinking nothing of tomorrow, let us allow nothing to entice us away from the rule of the monastery.

Chapter 31 - How no-one can overcome avarice without remaining in the monastery, and how one may become able to remain there.
Doubtless we shall never achieve this, nor be able to persevere under the rule of our order, unless the virtue of Patience be firmly grounded within us, a virtue which springs from no fount but humility. Humility can keep us free from anxiety, while patience enables us to bear any anxiety that may have arisen.

BOOK EIGHT

Of the Spirit of Wrath

Chapter 1 - How the fourth contest is with the vice of wrath, and what evils this passion generates.

In the fourth round of our contest, we must eradicate the deadly virus of wrath from the recesses of the soul. As long as this lurks in our hearts, and blinds our mind's eye with its evil darkness, we are incapable of acquiring the discretion to decide rightly, or of possessing a truly perceptive insight or mature judgement, and we are unable to participate in life, to hold on to justice, or even to perceive the true spiritual light, for "my eye is confounded by wrath". (*Psalm 30/1:10*) Nor can we become wise, however much we may appear so in the eyes of those who observe us, for "anger rests in the bosom of the unwise." (*Ecclus. 7:10 LXX*) Nor indeed can we attain eternal life, however sensible the judgement of men deem us to be, for "wrath destroys even the sensible". (*Prov. 15:1 LXX*) We will be unable to obtain the equilibrium of righteousness in a wise and discerning heart, however much we may be considered perfect and holy in the eyes of all, for "a man's anger does not work the righteousness of God". (*James 1:20*) Why, the very sobriety of dignity, which even men of this world customarily possess, is beyond our reach, even if we are reputed to be respectable and of good birth, for "a wrathful man is of no repute". (*Prov. 11:25 LXX*) We shall have no hope of acquiring mature deliberation, despite seeming to be serious and well able to discern, for "an angry man acts without deliberation." (*Prov. 14:17 LXX*) Nor indeed can we be free from disturbing anxiety, nor be clear from sin, even if no worries are brought upon us by others, for "a hot-tempered man stirs up strife, and a wrathful man uncovers sins." (*Prov. 29:22 LXX*)

Chapter 2 - On those who claim that anger is not wrong, if we are angry with the wicked, for even God is said to be angry.

We have heard that many try to excuse this dangerous disease of the soul, and justify it by a distorted interpretation of Scripture, when they say it is not wrong to be wrathful with our erring brethren. Why, they say, God himself is said to be wrathful and angry against those who refuse to understand or who condemn the wise. For instance "The Lord was wrath with his people", (*Psalm 105/6:40*) and the prophet prays, "Lord do not condemn me in your anger, nor punish me in your wrath." (*Psalm 6:2*) They do not understand that in trying to give men an excuse for a dangerous vice, they are insinuating that a wrongful earthly passion could be found in the infinite Divinity, the fount of all holiness.

Chapter 3 - Of how we attribute our own activities to God.

If we were to take these things literally when they are spoken about God, according to their earthly and carnal sense, then he must have been asleep, when we say, "Arise, why do you sleep, O Lord?" (*Psalm 43/4:23*) although elsewhere it says, "Lo, he sleeps not nor slumbers, Israel's guard." (*Psalm 120/1:4*) He must stand, or sit, since it says, "Heaven is my throne, and the earth the footstool beneath my feet," (*Isaiah 66:1 LXX*) although he "holds the heavens in the palm of his hands, and the earth is enclosed within his fist." (*Isaiah 40:12*) He must be inebriated with wine, for it says, "The Lord rose up like a man asleep, like a mighty one overcome with wine," (*Psalm 77:65*) he who "alone possesses immortality, and dwells in light inaccessible." (*I Tim. 6:16*) I shall pass over the ignorance and forgetfulness which we often find attributed to Him in Scripture, not to mention the specific parts of the body by which He is described as if He were in human form, that is to say hair, head and nostrils, eyes and face, hands and arms, fingers, a womb and feet - if we were to take these according to their common meaning, we would have to consider God to be composed of limbs and organs in bodily form, which it would be monstrous to assert, and far from our intention!

Chapter 4 - What we are to think of the human parts and passions attributed to the unchanging and incorporeal God.

Since we cannot understand these things literally without committing an unspeakable blasphemy against Him who is defined in Holy Writ as invisible, ineffable, incomprehensible, inestimable, simple and incomposite, so too the emotion of anger and wrath cannot be assigned to His unchangeable nature without gross blasphemy. By the metaphor of human parts we must understand the divine operation and vast activities of God, which cannot be conveyed to us except by these customary bodily images; for example by "mouth" we mean his utterances, which may be infused by grace into the unconscious mind, or which we recognise in the words of the Patriarchs and Prophets. By His "eyes" we understand His profound perception, which scrutinises and observes all things, and which misses nothing of what we do or are about to do or think. By the metaphor of "hands" we understand His providence and activity, for He is the creator and founder of all things. His "arms" represent His strength and control by which He sustains, directs and rules all things. And passing by other things, what does His "white hair" mean other than the divine length of days and great age? For He is without any beginning, before all times and prior to all creation.

In the same manner when we read about the wrath and anger of God we must understand this not anthropomorphically (that is, according to base human passions) but in a manner worthy of God who is free from all emotion. As we acknowledge Him to be the judge and avenger of all the wickedness worked in the world, the fearful chastiser of our actions, and we fear him as we use these words, we tremble to admit anything contrary to his will. For human nature usually fears those whom it sees to be wrathful, and avoids offending them, as on the part of the most equitable of judges their avenging wrath is fearful to those who have some crime on their consciences. It is not indeed because this passion resides in the minds of those who are to judge justly, but because that emotion which accompanies the execution of the law and the establishment of justice and equity is felt by those who thus fear. Hence no matter how mild the manner and gentle the bearing of those who pronounce sentence on their crime, those who deserve punishment consider it to be great wrath and savage anger. It would be a long task, and irrelevant to this book, to explain everything which is said of God in Holy Scripture using human metaphors. Enough has been said for our present purpose, which is about opposing the sin of anger, so that no one may now ignorantly find an excuse for this vice leading to eternal death, in the Scripture which brings us holiness in the healing salvation of eternal life.

Chapter 5 - How placid a monk ought to be.

Now a monk, who is aiming at perfection, and desires to compete legitimately in the spiritual contest, must be a stranger to all taint of anger and wrath, and listen to what the Vessel of Election said to him: "Let all anger, indignation, violence and blasphemy be eliminated from among you along with all ill-will." (*Eph. 4:31*) When he says, "let all anger be eliminated from among you", he makes no exception as if it could ever be needful or useful for us. When a brother sins, he is quick to apply the necessary cure in such a manner that he applies a remedy to the one suffering from what may be a slight affliction, but does not involve himself in the more dangerous sickness of blind anger. One who wishes to heal the wound of another should be healthy and free from all debilitating sickness, lest in the Gospel's words they say, "Physician, heal thyself!" (*Luke 4:23*) and lest he observe a speck in his brother's eye, without seeing the beam in his own eye; how will he be able to see to remove the speck from his brother's eye when he carries the beam of wrath in his own eye? (*Matth. 7:3-5*)

Chapter 6 - On justified and unjustified anger.

Whatever the reason for the passion of anger arising, it blinds the eyes of the mind, and puts a pernicious beam into the faculty of sight like a dangerous cataract, blocking the light of the sun of justice. It makes no difference whether our eyes are covered with a golden blindfold or one of lead, or any metal you choose; the value of the metal does not alter the quality of blindness.

Chapter 7 - The only occasion when anger is necessary for us. (This chapter division is not in Migne)
True, we have the healthy instinct of anger given us for a valid reason, for which alone it is useful and healthy to feel anger, that is when we are aroused to combat the evil passions of our own hearts, and are indignant that our secret thoughts turn to things which we would be ashamed to do or even speak of before men. In the presence of the angels, and in the sight of God who penetrates all things, we are afraid and tremble because nothing can remain hidden in our consciences.

Chapter 8 - How anger may be usefully employed, as we see the holy David did.
Indeed we may be indignant at anger itself, when it grows against our brother, and we may angrily drive out its deadly urgings, allowing it no hidden foothold in the depths of our hearts. The prophet teaches us to be angry in this sense, of driving anger out of his feelings so as not to desire retribution against his own enemies or those shown him by God, when he says, "be angry and sin not". *(Psalm 4:5)* For when David longed for some water from the cistern in Bethlehem, and it was brought to him by the heroes through enemy lines, he poured it out on the earth at once, offering it to the Lord to extinguish the passion of desire against which he was wrathful, refusing to indulge his yearnings. He said, "May the Lord be good to me because I have done this, for shall I drink the blood of these men who have brought it me, at the peril of their lives?" *(II Sam. 23:17)* And again when Shimei hurled stones and abuse at King David in his hearing, and his general Abishai the son of Zeruiah wanted to avenge the insult to the king by cutting off his head, the holy David was greatly indignant against his evil suggestion, and preserved his humility and patience unperturbed, mildly saying, "What does it matter to me and you, son of Zeruiah? Let him curse, if the Lord has told him to curse David. Who would dare to question why he does this? See, my own son, the

fruit of my loins, seeks my life; how much more this son of Benjamin! Leave him, let him curse at the Lord's command - perchance the Lord will look upon my affliction and render me good in return for the curses of today." (*II Sam. 16:10-12*)

Chapter 9 - On using anger against ourselves.
We are therefore commanded to be angry in a right sense, against our own selves and the evil thoughts that occur to us, and not to sin, that is not to let them come to effect. The following verse clearly explains what this means: "You that speak in your hearts, be smitten upon your beds." (*Psalm 4:5*) That is, whatever you imagine in your hearts, as sudden sly thoughts creep in, you should expel by wise consideration and eliminate all the turmoil and emotion of anger; as if lying quietly on your beds, improve and correct yourselves by a saving compunction. St Paul too quotes this verse as a witness, "Be angry and sin not", saying, "Let not the sun go down upon your anger, and give no place to the devil." (*Eph. 4:26*) If it is evil to let the sun set on our anger, and anger gives the devil immediate entrance into our hearts, how are we previously commanded to anger when it says "Be ye angry and sin not"? Does it not clearly mean to be angry with your vices and your wrath, lest Christ the Sun of Righteousness begin to set with your connivance because of the anger which darkens your minds, until with his departure you make space for the devil in your hearts?

Chapter 10 - Of which sun is it said that it should not go down on our anger.
The sun in question is clearly indicated by God speaking through the prophet who says, "The sun of justice will rise on those who fear my name, with healing in his wings." (*Mal. 4:2*) And again the prophet speaks of its setting at midday over sinners and false prophets, and those who are wrathful, "The sun sets on them at midday." (*Amos 8:9*) According to the allegorical sense, the sun represents the mind, understanding or reason, because it illuminates all the thoughts and decisions of the heart - now that should certainly not be extinguished by anger, for if it were eclipsed, our understanding would be totally

overwhelmed by the darkness of confusion along with its author the Devil, so that we would be so wrapt in the darkness of anger that we would not know at all what to do, as if plunged into thick night. This interpretation of the apostle's words was taught to us by the elders who trained us, for it is needful to recount what they thought about anger, even at this great length. They do not allow anger to overwhelm our hearts for an instant; as the Gospel says, "He who is angry with his brother is liable to judgement." (*Matth. 5:22*) Otherwise, if we were permitted to remain angry until sunset, our ill temper would be able to vent itself in fury and vengeance before the sun could sink to its setting.

Chapter 11 - Of those to whose anger not even the setting of this sun has put an end.

What can I say about those (whom I can only mention with shame) whose anger is not placated by sunset, but who sustain it for days, and retain rancour in their hearts against those who have provoked them? They may deny verbally that they are angry, but are shown up as really burning with wrath by their actions. For they do not address them with their usual speech, nor converse with them in their accustomed manner, and consider themselves to be no way to blame as long as they do not take steps to avenge themselves; that indeed they do not dare do openly, or are perhaps unable to, so that the poison of anger turns inward, to their own peril, and they silently brood over it, so that it devours them secretly, for they do not expel their sad bitterness at once but allow it to fester for many days till it dwindle in time.

Chapter 12 - That the aim of sorrow or anger is that a man should exercise it as far as he is able.

It is not the only possible outcome of anger, to carry its promptings to their natural conclusion, with the complete satisfaction of all wrath and grief; for we must also notice those who restrain their temper not through love of peace but through inability to avenge themselves. They are unable to do anything against those they are angry with, except to avoid their usual friendly conversation with them, as if wrath could only be exercised in violent action. We must not fail to pluck it out of our hearts, lest we be so blinded by its darkness that we fail to admit wise counsels or the light of knowledge, and are quite incapable of being the Temples of the Holy Spirit, for the spirit of wrath dwells within us. Anger concealed in the heart may not offend those who are near us, but excludes the bright radiance of the Holy Spirit as much as if it were displayed.

Chapter 13 - How we must not retain anger even for an instant.
The Lord forbids us to retain anger even for a moment, for he does not let us even offer the spiritual sacrifice of prayer if we are aware of nursing any bitterness against another; "If you are offering your gift at the altar, and there remember that your brother has any complaint against you, leave your gift there before the altar, go first to be reconciled with your brother, and then come and offer your gift." (*Matth. 5:23-4*) How therefore can we allow ourselves to keep a grievance against a brother even as long as until sunset today, let alone for several days, when we are not permitted to offer our prayers to God if anyone has something against us? For the Apostle bids us "Pray without ceasing," (*I Thess. 5:17*) and "In every place lift up pure hands, without wrath or deceit." (*I Tim. 2:8*) This means that we should either never pray as long as we retain this poison in our hearts, and thus be condemned at the Apostle's command, or that of the Gospel, that we should pray at all times and in all places; alternatively if we attempt to offer prayers against his command, deceiving ourselves, we would be found to be offering not prayer to the Lord but a spirit of obstinate rebellion to him.

Chapter 14 - On brotherly reconciliation.
Since we often treat our wounded and saddened brothers with contempt, or despise them, saying that it is not our fault that they are aggrieved, He who is the physician of souls and the observer of secrets, who wishes to eradicate the seeds of wrath from our hearts,

not only commands us to forgive if we are offended, and to be reconciled with our brethren, till no memory remain of our grievance or bitterness against them, but He also gives us a similar commandment, if we know of any complaint they have against us, whether justified or not, to leave our gift before the altar - that is to defer our prayer - until we have hurried to offer them amends, and only after receiving our brother's forgiveness, to offer the sacrifice of our prayers. For the Lord of all is not pleased with our worship if what He receives from one He loses from another who is overwhelmed with grief. If one is injured, all suffer loss, for He desires and expects the salvation of all His servants in the same way. Thus if our brother has something against us, our prayer will be of no avail, just as much as if we were nursing bitter indignation in a spirit of pride.

Chapter 15 - How even the Old Law reproves anger in thought as well as effect.
We need not confine ourselves to the teaching of the Gospels and Epistles, for even the Old Testament, which may seem to be less strict, does give the same commandment, saying, "Do not hate your brother in your heart", and again, "Do not remember when your fellow citizens offend you", and again, "The paths of those who remember injuries lead to the grave." (*Lev. 19:17-18*) So you see that the sin lies not just in actions but even in our secret thoughts, since we are commanded to pluck up hatred from the heart, and forbear not just the performance of vengeance but even the thought of it.

Chapter 16 - Of the uselessness of monastic life if we do not renounce our evil ways.
If we find ourselves overcome by pride and intolerance, and would like to correct our disordered and sinful ways, we may protest that we need solitude, as if we could discover the virtue of patience there, where no one would disturb us. We make excuses for our negligence, and assert that we are upset not by our own impatience but through our brothers' fault. As long as we attribute to others the causes of our

weakness, we will never succeed in reaching our goal of perfect patience.

Chapter 17 - How peace of mind is found not through the will of others but is within our own power.
This goal of peaceful improvement cannot be reached through the decisions of others, which is forever beyond our control, but is found rather in our own attitude. To be free from wrath is not dependent on the perfection of others, but stems from our own virtue, which is acquired through our own tolerance, not other people's patience.

Chapter 18 - What should be our intention in seeking solitude, and what progress made there.
Only those who are perfect and free from all sin should seek solitude, once their faults have been boiled out of them in community life; they should enter the desert not as an escape for the weak, but through longing for the contemplation of God, and the desire of a greater insight, which cannot be found except in solitude by those who are perfect. For if we bring any unhealed vices into the desert with us, we shall find that they have not been abolished but are quite manifest. For though solitude is able to bring the purest contemplation to those who are free from sin, and to reveal the knowledge of spiritual secrets to the incorrupt mind, yet to those who have not amended their lives, solitude tends not just to preserve but to aggravate vices. A man may seem to be patient and humble, until he is deprived of human company, when he will quickly revert to type as soon as any inconvenience gives him cause, and the hidden vices will rapidly emerge, and break out more fiercely, like unbridled horses, fresh after a long rest, bolting from their stalls to the great peril of their driver. Our vices become more obvious when we are deprived of the company of men, unless they are already purged, and if we sit still in solitude we would find ourselves without even that shadow of patience which we gave the appearance of possessing while we lived with the brothers, if only out of respect for them and our own reputation.

Chapter 19 - How we should assess those who are patient only when no one provokes them.

The various types of poisonous snake and venomous beast are no less dangerous when they are alone in their desert lairs, and are not called safe just because they are not harming anyone, which is the result not of an onset of goodwill, but of sheer necessity, being isolated. When they get a chance of harming anyone they do so at once, revealing the poison hidden within them and their fierce nature. In the same way it is not enough for those seeking perfection to refrain from anger against men. We can remember during our time in the desert becoming vexed with a pen, whether it were too fine or too broad; with the penknife, whose edge was too blunt to cut cleanly; with a tinderbox, when perhaps we were eager to begin reading and it took a long time to strike a spark; and the emotion of indignation arose till we were unable to assuage or allay our passionate anger except against material objects, or against the Devil who had cursed them. Therefore to acquire perfection it is not sufficient to stay away from men who might provoke our anger, for if we have not already gained patience that same passion of anger may be aroused against dumb objects [and trivial occurrences]. If anger lurks in the heart it will not allow us to enjoy a state of unbroken calm, nor to rid ourselves of other vices; unless we somehow imagine we can turn our emotions to profit, in as much as dumb inanimate objects make no response to our curses and passion, and therefore cannot provoke our temper to break out in even greater wrath.

Chapter 20 - How the Gospel teaches us to cut anger away.

Now if we want to gain that pitch of perfection and its divine reward, as it is said, "Blessed are the clean of heart, for they shall see God," (*Matth. 5:8*) we must not only eliminate anger from our actions, but also eradicate it from our thoughts. There is not much point in restraining words of wrath, or violent deeds, if God from whom no secrets are hid can see anger in our hearts. The Gospel teaches us to cut away the very roots of vice more than its fruits, for they will never grow again once the roots have been torn up. The mind can truly persevere in holiness and patience once this vice has been uprooted from the depths of our hearts, not just from our superficial words and works. To stop us committing murder, we must cut away anger and hatred, for the crime of murder could never be conceived without them. "He who is angry with his brother is answerable to the court", and "he who hates his brother is a murderer." (*Matth. 5:22; I John 3:15*) Since he longs in his heart to kill, although in the eyes of men his hand and sword have not been seen to shed blood, in the eyes of the Lord his anger convicts him of murder. God gives each man his reward or punishment, not only for actions put into effect, but also for His desires and aspirations, as He says through the prophet: "I will come and collect together the works and thoughts of all nations and languages"; (*Isaiah 66:18*) and St Paul adds, "it is their thoughts that will accuse them or acquit them on the day when God will judge the hidden things of men." (*Rom. 2:15-16*)

Chapter 21 - Whether when the Gospel says "he who is angry with his brother..." etc, we should read in addition "without cause."

We must understand that when in some copies of the Gospels we find "he who is angry with his brother *without cause* will be liable to condemnation", (*Matth. 5:22*) the "without cause" is an interpolation added by those who see no reason to renounce anger over a just cause, for no one will admit that he is angry without cause no matter what the reason for his wrath. That proves that it is an addition, made by those who fail to understand that Scripture intends to eradicate the root of anger totally, and to preserve no excuse for indignation; for if we were bidden to be angry "with good cause" we would find ourselves a pretext for anger "without cause." The fruit of patience is not in righteous anger but in not being angry at all. Granted that some interpret the "without cause" as meaning that he is said to be angry "without cause" when he is not permitted to take vengeance on the butt of his anger, but it is better to take it as it is found written in many modern copies and all the older ones.

Chapter 22 - The remedy by which we may eradicate anger from our hearts.

An athlete of Christ who competes lawfully must eradicate the emotion of anger. The best remedy for this disease is to begin by believing that we are never justified in being angry, whether for a good or bad reason, understanding that we would quickly lose any light of discernment, any steadfastness of purpose, honour itself and the guidance of righteousness, if the principal light of our hearts were shrouded in such darkness. Moreover, while the spirit of wrath dwells in our hearts the purity of our minds would be disturbed, and we could never become temples of the Holy Spirit. Finally, we should consider that we could not even lawfully pray if the prayers we offered to God were ill tempered. Keeping the uncertain state of man ever before our eyes, let us believe ourselves daily to be on the point of death, and know that we would profit nothing from pure chastity, the renunciation of all our property, the contempt of riches, fasting or vigils, for the Universal Judge has promised eternal punishment for wrath and hatred alone.

BOOK NINE

On the Spirit of Melancholy

Chapter 1 - That our fifth round is against the spirit of Melancholy; and on the damage it does to the mind.
In our fifth round we must fend off the attacks of morbid melancholy. If that can once gain the mastery over our hearts, through individual occurrences, and unspecified chances, it will eventually cut us off from any insight of divine contemplation, and cast the mind down from its general state of purity to weaken it and to depress it. It does not suffer us to complete our prayer with the usual mental alertness, allows no healing to come through spiritual reading, prevents us from being peaceful or at ease with our brethren, and makes us impatient and touchy in all our manual or divine work. When all sound discernment is lost, and the heart is worried and perturbed, it makes us all but distracted and dazed, and breaks us with overwhelming gloom.

Chapter 2 - The cure for the disease of melancholy.
To cure this disease we must take precautions no less than in other cases if we desire to put legitimate effort into our spiritual competition. For "just as moths destroy clothing and worms wood, so melancholy destroys the heart of man." (*Prov. 25:20*) The Holy Spirit has shown clearly enough how dangerous this pernicious vice can be.

Chapter 3 - What a soul is like when it is being devoured by melancholy.
When a garment has been attacked by moth it has no further value or honourable use; it is the same with wood which is riddled with worm, it is no use for decoration or building but is fit only to be burnt. So too with the soul, eaten up with the attacks of devouring gloom, it is useless. It cannot serve for the High Priest's vestments, of which David sings that the anointing of the Holy Spirit descends from

Heaven, first onto Aaron's beard and then onto the border of his vestments, thus, "Like ointment on the head which flows down to the beard of Aaron, which reaches to the border of his robe." (*Psalm 132/3:2*) Nor can it be useful for building and adorning that spiritual temple, of which Paul laid the foundation like a skilled architect, saying, "You are the Temple of God, and the Spirit of God dwells in you;" (*I Cor. 3:16, 6:16*) whose timber is such as the bride describes in the Song of Songs, "Our beams are of cypress, the boards of our house are cedar." (*Song 1:16 LXX*) These types of wood were chosen for the temple of God because they are sweet-smelling and incorruptible, so that they neither decay through age nor are subject to the ravages of worm.

Chapter 4 - How and where melancholy arises.
Melancholy often follows on the preceding vice, anger, and can also arise from failing to acquire what avarice yearns for, when we find we have failed to attain what we have been hoping for. But sometimes it arises for no apparent cause which might provoke us to such depths, but we are cast down by the enemy's insinuations, and oppressed by such sudden sadness that we are unable to welcome even our nearest and best beloved with our usual cheerfulness, and whatever conversation they make with us, we find irrelevant and unwanted. We can give them no pleasant answer, while our whole hearts are tainted with the bitterness of melancholy.

Chapter 5 - That it is not other peoples' fault but our own if we are disturbed.
You can see very clearly that when disturbing emotions arise in us it is not always the fault of others, but our own, for we have the germs of offence and the seeds of vice hidden within ourselves, so that when the dew of temptation waters the mind, they spring up at once into branches and fruits.

Chapter 6 - How one does not collapse after a sudden shock, but dwindles little by little through brooding over long grievances.

No one is ever so wounded by another's fault that he is compelled to sin, unless he had the evil inclination already in his heart. Nor should we believe that anyone is so suddenly ensnared that he is plunged into the depths of carnal lust merely on catching sight of a woman; it is rather that the chance sight brings into the open the hidden depravity of the secret soul.

Chapter 7 - That we should not shun the company of the brethren in order to acquire perfection, but that we must be careful to cultivate patience.

God, the creator of all, knows better than anyone how to heal His handiwork, and since the roots of sin lie within ourselves, not in others, He does not advise us to shun the company of our brethren, nor to avoid those whom we imagine we have harmed, or to have harmed us, but He commands us to mix with them, knowing that a perfect heart is not gained by separation from men but through the virtue of patience. Once we have that, it can preserve us at peace in the midst of those who hate peace, just as if we do not possess it, we will be quarrelsome even among those who are perfect and superior to ourselves. It is impossible in human intercourse to avoid all disturbing occasions, which might provoke us to desert our comrades, so that since we cannot avoid things that cause sadness and might drive us apart, let us change them.

Chapter 8 - If we have once amended our own behaviour, we could be at peace with anyone.

Therefore we must take care to correct our morals and behaviour urgently. Once they are improved, we will easily get on not only with men but even with wild beasts, as we hear in the book of Job, "The beasts of the earth will be at peace with thee." (*Job 5:23 LXX*) We shall not be afraid of being offended by external events, nor could anything from outside cause us to stumble, if we do not allow the roots of sin to be established within us. "For there will be high peace for those who love thy law, O Lord, and nothing shall make them to stumble." (*Psalm 118/9:165*)

Chapter 9 - Of another type of melancholy which causes us to despair of salvation.
 There is another even more pernicious type of melancholy, which does not lead the suffering soul to improvement of life nor the correction of vices, but to utter despair. This is what prevented Cain from repentance after the murder of his brother, and Judas after his betrayal, who did not rush to repent and be saved but in his despair resorted to the noose.

Chapter 10 - The only way in which sadness can be beneficial.
The only manner in which sadness can be considered beneficial is when it comes to us through sorrow for our sins, the desire of perfection, or the consideration of future bliss. St Paul writes of this, "Sorrow which is according to God works penance unto a sure salvation; while the sorrow of this world works death." (*II Cor. 7:10*)

Chapter 11 - How to distinguish a useful sorrow that comes from God, from one that is devilish and deadly.
That sorrow which works penance unto salvation shows that it derives from the love of God in that it is obedient, genial, humble, docile, even tempered and patient; it tirelessly applies itself to every sort of physical mortification and contrition of spirit, in its longing for perfection; it grows with a certain joy in hope of progress, and maintains that affable and tolerant even temper, for it contains within itself all the fruits of the Holy Spirit, as the Apostle enumerates them: "The fruits of the Spirit are charity, joy, peace, tolerance, goodness, kindness, faith, mildness and self-control." (*Gal. 5:22-3*) Melancholy on the other hand is harsh, intolerant, cruel, full of rancour and futile gloom, suffering in despair. When it seizes a man it breaks him and drags him away from any useful or salutary grief; being quite unreasonable it not only hinders him from efficacious prayer but even loses him all those fruits of the spirit which we have listed, knowing that prayer would have conferred them.

Chapter 12 - How, apart from that saving sorrow, which arises in three ways, all melancholy must be resisted as being dangerous.

Therefore, apart from that sorrow which arises for the sake of saving penance, or from the desire of perfection, or the longing for what is to come, all melancholy must be equally resisted, being worldly and pernicious, and quite excluded from our hearts no less than we do the spirits of fornication, avarice and wrath.

Chapter 13 - The remedies by which we may drive melancholy out of our hearts.
Now this is how to drive this deadly emotion away from ourselves: we must build up the mind with meditation on divine things, and fill it with the thought of hope for the future, and the consideration of our promised bliss. In this way we shall be strong enough to overcome all types of melancholy, whether they arise from anger beforehand, or through the loss of property or some injury done to us; or are caused by some wrong we have suffered or spring from an irrational mental anxiety or bring upon us a deadly despair. In the prospect of eternity and our reward to come we shall always be joyful and remain steadfast, neither cast down by present misfortune, nor elated by good chance, but considering both to be temporary and soon to pass.

BOOK TEN

Of the Spirit of Depression

Chapter 1 - How our sixth round is against the spirit of Depression, and what of its nature.

Our sixth struggle is against what the Greeks call *accedia* and which we may call listlessness or depression. It is similar to melancholy, and especially prevalent among pilgrims and hermits, a common and dangerous enemy to those who live in the desert. It particularly troubles a monk at midday, like a malaria which recurs at regular intervals, as the infection brings burning fevers on the suffering soul at predictable set times. Many of the elders consider this to be the "noonday devil" which is mentioned in the ninetieth psalm.

Chapter 2 - How depression seeps into the heart of a monk, and the injury it inflicts on the mind.

When depression attacks the wretched monk, it engenders a loathing for his situation, dislike of his cell, and contemptuous disparagement of his brethren, whether they live with him or at a distance, as if they were lax and unspiritual. It makes him desultory and lazy at any task to be done within the walls of his cell. It does not let him sit in his cell, and apply himself to his duty of reading; he grumbles that he has frequently spent such a long time at this exercise and profited nothing; he complains with sighs that he can gain no spiritual benefit as long as he is tied to such company; he laments that he is quite void of any spiritual advancement, and stagnates in this futile place; although he is capable of governing others to their great advantage, he has made no foundation, and no one is profiting from his training and instruction. He makes much of monasteries that are situated afar off, and talks about their more advantageous positions and healthier sites. He describes the community of brothers there, how friendly and how deeply spiritual they are; while in contrast everything to hand is disagreeable; not only are the brothers living in this place quite disedifying, but it is impossible to make a living here without enormous effort. In fine, he considers he cannot be saved if he stays where he is, and he must leave this cell which would be the death of him if he stayed in it, and take himself off as soon as possible. And then the middle of the day brings such physical weariness and hunger that he looks exhausted as if by a long journey or heavy labour, or seems half starved, as if deprived of food for two or three days. He looks anxiously this way and that, unhappy because no brother is coming to see him; he goes in and out of his cell and continually looks at the sun as if it were slow in setting. Thus in an unreasonable mental turmoil, as if overwhelmed in gloomy darkness, he becomes idle and empty of any spiritual work, until he thinks he can find no cure for this weariness except in visiting some brother, or else in the easy consolation of sleep. The disease suggests that it would be permissible, nay necessary, to exchange greetings with the brethren, to visit the sick, even far off at a distance. Then he decides it would be a devout religious work to ask after his relations, including female ones, and to rush over to greet them often; and that it would be a gesture of great devotion to make frequent visits to that devout and pious lady who is destitute without any support from her family - it would be a holy work to provide for her necessities since her own people have neglected and ignored her, and it would be better to spend one's effort in these good works than to sit in a cell without profit or progress.

Chapter 3 - What sort of attacks depression makes on a monk.
Thus the unhappy soul is vexed and assaulted by these wiles of the enemy, as if it were being battered by a weighty ram, until it gives in to sloth, or becomes used to leaving the enclosure of the cell and finding consolation from this burden in visiting other monks. What it uses as an immediate remedy soon becomes a dangerous complaint in itself. For the adversary will assault the victim more often and more severely, once he knows that he will turn his back if engaged in close con-

flict, and sees that he puts his hope only in flight, not in victory or resistance; thus little by little he draws him from the cell, till he begins to forget that the obligation of his profession is no more than the wrapt contemplation of that divine purity which exceeds all things, and which cannot be found anywhere except in silence and in remaining constantly in the cell in meditation. Once the soldier of Christ has abandoned his colours and deserted, and involved himself in secular business, he cannot please the master he had promised to serve.

Chapter 4 - How depression blinds the mind against any consideration of virtue.
The holy David well expressed the great evils of this complaint in one verse: "My soul is asleep for very weariness," *(Psalm 118/19:28)* that is, through depression. He rightly says not the "body" but the "soul" is asleep. For truly the soul sleeps, unaware of any contemplation of virtue or spiritual insight, once it is damaged by the onset of this disease.

Chapter 5 - How the struggle against accedia is twofold.
Now the true athlete of Christ, who longs to compete legitimately in the contest for perfection, will be swift to purge this disease out of the recesses of his soul, and will struggle against this pernicious spirit of accedia on all sides. He will not succumb to the lure of sleep, nor quit the monastic enclosure and become a deserter on any speciously pious pretext whatever.

Chapter 6 - How far may fall those whom depression defeats.
Whenever accedia begins to overwhelm anyone in any way, he either suffers languor and inertia and remains in his cell with no spiritual benefit, or else he departs from the cell and becomes thereafter unstable, wandering about, useless for anything, and constantly going around the cells and monasteries of other brethren, for no other purpose than to anticipate some future possibility of entertainment, on whatever excuse. For the slothful mind sees no other goal than food and drink, until it finds the companionship of some man, or

woman, languishing under the same ennui, and becomes involved in their needs and interests. Gradually he is entangled in evil practices, and, as if he were constricted by a coiling serpent, will never again extricate himself and return to his former holy profession.

Chapter 7 - St Paul's advice on the spirit of depression.
The Holy Apostle Paul, being a true doctor of the spirit, was instructed by the Holy Spirit to discern the evil which arises from a spirit of accedia, when it first creeps in or when it lies hid among the monks, and is quick to offer healing remedies in his teaching. Writing to the Thessalonicans, as an experienced and skilful doctor, at first he treats his patients' ills with soothing and gentle words. Beginning in charity he praises them up to a point, until the deadly virus is mollified by such easy remedies, and the swelling of indignation has abated, and they become capable of enduring the more drastic remedy: "About brotherly charity I have no need to write to you, for you have learnt this yourselves from God, that you should love one another. You display this love moreover to all the brothers throughout Macedon." (*I Thess. 4:9-10*) He begins with a soothing poultice of praise, and woos their ears to be open to the healing word which will cure them. He applies it again: "We beseech you, brethren, that you be more generous still." (*ibid., v. 10*) He lulls them with his gentle way of speech, so as not to deter them from listening to their complete cure. Why, O Apostle, do you ask that they be more generous still, that is to say generous in charity, when you have already said, "About brotherly charity I have no need to write to you"? Why is it needful for you to write, "We beseech you, brethren, that you be more generous still", when in this matter they had no need for anything to be written to them? For you yourself give the reason why they do not need it, saying, "you have learnt this yourselves from God, that you should love one another." And you add a third and greater point, in that they are not only taught by God but even carry out the lesson they had learnt. "You display this love, moreover", not only towards one or two, but "to all the brothers", not only to your fellow citizens and

friends, but "throughout Macedon."

Say, therefore, what this is all leading to. He continues, "We beseech you, brethren, that you be more generous still", and he has scarcely built them up before he shatters them: "See to it that you be at peace." He has begun by naming the problem. Secondly he says, "and that you go about your business," and a third point, "that you work with your hands just as we taught you." Fourthly, "that you behave decently towards those outside," and fifthly, "that you covet no one else's goods." Here we can see how he has built up slowly, delaying until after that preface to speak of what he had in mind to say. "See to it that you be at peace", that is, that you stay in your cells, and are not disturbed by various rumours such as idle tales and wishes generate, and spread such disturbance among others. "Go about your business", not eager in your curiosity to find out about the doings of the world, and to hear the opinions of many, giving your attention not to your own improvement or the love of virtue, but to running down your brethren. "Work with your hands just as we taught you." To preserve you against what you were warned against doing above, that is being disturbed and anxious about others' affairs, or behaving badly towards those outside or coveting the goods of others, he inveighs in the words, "work with your hands just as we taught you." He makes it clear that idleness is the cause of those things he has just warned us against. No one can be worried, or anxious about the affairs of others, unless he has failed to devote himself to his manual work. His fourth point was to specify the disease which arises from idleness, that is behaving badly, when he says, "behave decently towards those outside." No one can behave decently, even towards men of this world, if he is discontented with his enclosure and with performing manual tasks; he is bound to behave badly just in the search for a living, and to be eager for admiration, running after new ideas, looking for opportunities for gossip and news, to give himself an opening and excuse to visit different homes. "And covet no one else's goods." If you are unhappy with the holy peaceful labour of your hands to earn your daily bread, you will be bound to yearn after gifts and endowments from others.

Do you see what serious and shameful problems arise from the single fault of idleness? That is why the very ones that St Paul soothes with gentle words in his earlier Epistle, he goes on to tackle with harsh and extreme remedies, since they have not profited by the gentle ones. No longer does he apply bland poultices of smooth words, no longer soft and gracious speech, no longer, "we request you, brothers," but, "we command you, brethren, in the name of Our Lord Jesus Christ, to withdraw from any brother who behaves badly". (*II Thess. 3:6*) First he requests, then he commands. First an appearance of mildness, then harsh and threatening orders. "We command you, brethren"; if you have not deigned to listen to our former request, now at least obey our orders. And the command is not made in simple words, but rendered terrible with the invocation of Our Lord Jesus Christ, lest they still ignore it as if it were only dependent on a human will, and consider it not worth observing strictly. Like an experienced doctor treating gangrenous limbs which have not responded to gentle medicine, he attempts a cure with a cut from the spiritual scalpel: "withdraw from any brother who behaves badly, and not according to the tradition which they had received from us."

Thus he bids them shun those who are unwilling to give time to labour, and to cut them off like limbs gangrenous with disuse, lest the sickness of sloth, like a deadly virus, spread insidiously into the healthy parts of the body. He goes on to say that those who will not work with their hands should eat their bread in silence, for he commands that the others should avoid them. Listen now to what reproaches he lays on them: firstly he calls them "disorderly", and "not behaving according to the tradition"; in other places he calls them "disobedient", since they are not prepared to do as he had instructed them, and "disreputable", since they do not observe the right and proper time for going out, visiting the sick, and speaking opportunely. The disorderly are bound to fall into all these vices, "not according to the tradition which they had received from us." He calls them contemptuous rebels, since they despise observing the tradition they had received from him, and were unwilling to imitate what they knew their teacher had not only spoken about but even put into practice, "for you know well how you ought to imitate us." (*II Thess. 3:7*) He piles up a great heap of reproaches when he asserts that they do not observe what they remember full well and had not only learnt to imitate through his verbal teaching but had even undertaken to perform at his example.

Chapter 8 - How he who is discontented with manual labour is bound to be contentious.

"For we were not contentious among you"; he demonstrates that he had not been contentious among them because he had been working, and clearly shows that the idle would always be contentious. "Nor did we eat anyone's bread for nothing"; the Teacher of the Gentiles makes his rebuke stronger with every word. (*II Thess. 3:8*) He who proclaimed the Gospel says he never accepted bread from anyone for nothing, although he knew that Our Lord had bidden that those "who preach the Gospel should live by the Gospel", (*I Cor. 9:14*) and also "The labourer is worthy of his hire." (*Matth. 10:10*) So if he did not accept his own food for nothing, despite the Lord's authorisation, though he was preaching the Gospel and performing such a sublime and spiritual work, how are we to behave, we who have not been commissioned to proclaim the Gospel, and have no obligation at all save only the salvation of our own souls? How can we dare to eat our bread for nothing with idle hands, when the Vessel of Election, burdened with the anxiety of proclaiming the Gospel, did not presume to eat without working? "In labour and toil," he says, "we worked night and day, so as not to burden you." (*II Thess. 3:8*) Thus he adds weight to his rebuke. He does not simply say that "we did not accept bread for nothing from any of you", and stop there, since he might have been understood to have lived on his own unearned invested income, or on subscriptions and gifts from other people, not them; but he says, "in labour and toil we worked night and day," that is we were supported by our own personal labour. This he says he did not through his own choice, or for amusement, to refresh and exercise the body, but because need and poverty obliged him to it, and not without great bodily fatigue. For it was not only during the hours of daylight that he pursued his occupation, but his need to make a living kept him working even at night, which might be thought more appropriate for rest.

Chapter 9 - How not only the Apostle but his companions also worked with their hands.

He tells us that it was not he alone who was thus dedicated, lest the example appear to apply only to one particular case, but he asserts that all those who accompanied him in preaching the Gospel worked in the same way, that is Silvanus and Timothy, who wrote these things jointly with him. When he says, "not to be a burden on any of you", he puts them to great shame. For if he, who proclaimed the Gospel, and commended it with signs and wonders, would not dare to eat his bread for nothing, lest he be a burden, how great a burden must they think themselves if they take their bread every day in idleness and sloth?

Chapter 10 - How the Apostle worked with his hands in order to give us an example.

"It is not as if we did not have the authority, but that we wish to give you an example to imitate." (*II Thess. 3:9*) Here he reveals the reason for undertaking such labour, "to give you an example to imitate." Maybe you could forget the teaching which he had so frequently dinned into your ears, but you would be sure to remember the example of his way of life which the evidence of your eyes recalls. This is no small rebuke to them, to say that he undertook this work, in weariness by day and by night, just to be an example to them. How stubborn they were in learning this, although for their sake he accepted this great burden without needing to. Although as he says, "I did have the authority", which I knew the Lord had promised me, to draw on all your possessions and wealth for my use, but I did not use this authority, lest what would be right and lawful for me should become an excuse for the laziness of others. Therefore, when preaching the Gospel, I preferred to support myself by the work of my own hands, to open a path of perfection for you as well, in your desire to follow the way of virtue, and to supply an example of conduct through my own work.

Chapter 11 - How he teaches us to work, not only by example but in words as well.
Now if he had kept silent about his work, his aim of instructing them by example might have had only little effect in training them in his commandments, so he continues, saying, "When we were with you we commanded you that he who was unwilling to work should not eat." (*II Thess. 3:10*) When they knew full well that he was a teacher of sound doctrine and instruction, and worked with his hands for the sake of training them, their idleness showed their contempt of him - this he demonstrates as well as his own careful concern, when he says that he gave them this example while he was with them, and also stressed it in his saying, that "he who is unwilling to work should not eat."

Chapter 12 - On the Apostle's saying, "He who will not work should not eat."
No longer does he address them in the language of doctor or physician, but he inveighs against them with the ruling of a stern judge. Using his full apostolic authority, he gives sentence against them as if they stood in contempt of court; the authority, I mean, which he claims to have received from the Lord when he writes threateningly to the Corinthians, where he warns those who are in a state of sin to be quick to reform themselves before his arrival, saying, "I beseech you not to make me use against you the full authority which has been given to me." (*II Cor. 10:2*) And again, "I would not be ashamed to assert the authority which the Lord gave me for your edification, not for your destruction." (*ibid, v. 8*) It is by that authority, you see, that he says, "he who is unwilling to work should not eat." He does not threaten them with an earthly sword, but the authority of the Holy Spirit, in forbidding them sustenance in this life. Maybe they would think little of the punishment of death in the distant future, and

still continue to be contemptuous in their love of ease, but if they were constrained by physical need and fear of imminent death, they would accept the teaching that saves them.

Chapter 13 - How he says "we hear there are some among you who are behaving badly".
After that severe but evangelical decree, he goes on to give the reason for what went before: "We have heard that there are some among you who behave badly, doing nothing, but only meddling." (*II Thess. 3:11*) He is not satisfied with diagnosing those who will not work as suffering from only one vice, for earlier in the Epistle he called them "disorderly", and "not behaving according to the tradition which they had received from him"; now he says they "behave badly" and "eat their bread for nothing." And here again, "we have heard that there are some among you who behave badly", and he continues at once with the second failing which is the cause of this disturbance, "doing nothing", and the third vice which sprouts from these, "but meddling."

Chapter 14 - How manual labour cuts off many vices.
He is quick to apply the appropriate remedy for such a growth of vice, and lays aside the apostolic authority which he had been using just before, to resume the compassion of a loving father or gentle doctor. He confers on his sons, or rather his patients, professional advice for healing, saying "We call on those who are thus affected, and we entreat them in the name of Our Lord Jesus, to work quietly and so earn their bread." (*II Thess. 3:12*) Like a skilled doctor, with a single piece of healthy advice, he treats the cause of so many ulcers which erupt from the infection of idleness. He well knows that the other evil effects which arise from the same disease will be effectively eliminated, once the original infection has been cured.

Chapter 15 - How kindly he deals with the idle and the careless.
Consistently acting like a wise and discerning doctor, he does not only strive to cure the ills of those who suffer, but also to preserve the well

in their good health, and gives them similar useful advice, saying, "Do not cease to do good"; (*II Thess. 3:13*) follow us, that is our way of life; fulfil the pattern given to you by imitating our labour, never copy their lazy inertia. "Do not cease to do good", which is to display kindness towards those who may have failed to observe what we had commanded. While he chastises the weak, lest they spend their time in idle disturbance and meddling, he also urges the strong not to fail in that kindness which Our Lord commands us to show to good and bad alike, even if the wicked are slow to return to the sound teaching. Rather they should do good to them and encourage them with consoling words of advice, and continue to give them kindness and help.

Chapter 16 - How we should correct sinners through love, not hatred.
Now, lest they should take advantage of this gentleness, and scorn to obey his commands, he again introduces his apostolic firmness: "And if anyone does not obey our command, write to me about him, and avoid his company so that he will put to shame." (*II Thess. 3:14*) He admonishes them by his own dignity and the public good on what to do, and how carefully they should obey the apostolic decrees, and then immediately adds a father's gentle kindness to show his sons what brotherly affection they should display towards the wayward, telling them, "not to treat anyone as an enemy, but to treat them as brethren." He mingles fatherly affection with severity, moderating the sentence which his apostolic zeal pronounced with gentle compassion. He bids them inform him about those who scorn to obey his commands, and to avoid their company, but he tells them to do this not in hatred, which is a vice, but in love of their brethren and hope for their improvement. "Avoid his company so that he will be put to shame", so that if he will not reform at my mild commands, at least he will be daunted by your all avoiding him in public, and eventually begin again to return to the path of salvation.

Chapter 17 - More texts in which St Paul bids us work and shows how he himself used to work.

He also talks about work in the Epistle to the Ephesians, saying, "Let he who was a thief steal no more, but let him do honest work with his hands so that he will have the means to give sustenance to the poor." (*Eph. 4:28*) We find him too in the Acts of the Apostles not only teaching the like but putting it into practice, for when he arrived in Corinth he would not stay anywhere but with Aquila and Priscilla, because they were skilled in the same craft in which he usually worked. This is the text: "After that, Paul left Athens and came to Corinth, where he met a Jew called Aquila, of Pontic origin, and his wife Priscilla. He visited and stayed with them, for they were of the same craft, and they worked together. Their trade was that of tentmaker." (*Acts 18:1-3*)

Chapter 18 - How the apostle worked sufficiently for his own needs and also for those of his companions.

When he came to Miletus, and sent from there to Ephesus, calling to himself the priests of the Ephesian Church to instruct them on how to govern the Church of God in his absence, he said, "I have not coveted the gold or silver of anyone; you know well that all my needs and those of my companions were met at my own hands. I have revealed all this to you, how you should work like this with your hands to relieve the sick, and remember the words of the Lord Jesus who said it is more blessed to give than to receive." (*Acts 20:33-5*) He left us a splendid pattern in his way of life when he demonstrates that he did not only work sufficiently to fulfil his own physical needs, but also met the needs of those who accompanied him; that is those who were so busy with the daily work of the ministry that they were quite unable to earn their own living with their hands in the same way. Just as he told the Thessalonicans that he worked in order to give them an example to imitate, so here he adds something, saying, "I have revealed all this to you, how you should work like this with your hands to relieve the sick", both in mind and body. That is, we should be quick to help them through our own effort and the profit of our own toil, rather than out of savings or investments, or other peoples' generous donations.

Chapter 19 - How we should understand "It is more blessed to give than to receive."

This also he says was a command of the Lord, citing the words of the Lord Jesus who said, "it is more blessed to give than to receive." (*Acts 20:35*) This means that the abundance of the giver is more blessed than the poverty of the recipient, when the gift depends not on money that had been hoarded up through insecurity and mistrust of the future, nor on the concealed investments of greed, but on honest toil and the product of one's own work. Then it is "more blessed to give than to receive", when the one who gives shares the poverty of the one who receives, and still is eager not only to supply his own needs, but to have enough to give charitably to the poor out of his own earnings. He is endowed with a twofold grace, in following the complete poverty of Christ by renouncing all his former property, as well as displaying a rich man's largesse through his own efforts. One man honours God by his honest work and by distributing the fruits of his honesty; while another is sunk in the sluggish inertia of idleness and on the Apostle's word shows himself unworthy even to eat bread, for if he remains idle contrary to that command, he could not accept food without being guilty of the sin of disobedience.

Chapter 20 - Of the idle monk who encouraged others to leave the monastery.

We knew of a monk (whom we could name if it would be of any benefit to know it) who while he lived in the monastery, and was obliged to hand over to the bursar every day his allotted produce, was afraid that he might become overstretched with a greater burden of work because someone else was producing more, or at least be embarrassed by that example. Hence, when he saw a new monk entering the monastery, who was willing to complete a greater quantity of work in faithful zeal, he would try secretly to dissuade him from this intention, and if he failed in that would persuade him to leave the community by his wicked advice and insinuations. To make him leave the more readily, he would pretend that he also was unhappy about many things, and wanted to depart, if only he could find a congenial companion in his flight. Once he had gained his consent, through his secretly disparaging the monastery, he would appoint a time to escape from the enclosure, or a place where the other could wait to meet him, pretending that he would follow close behind. The other would be so ashamed of his departure that he would not dare to apply again to the community from which he had fled, while the wretched author of his loss would sit tight in the monastery. A single example of this sort of man is enough to warn those who are beginners, and to make it abundantly clear how much evil idleness breeds in a monk, as Scripture says, (*Ecclus. 33:29*) as well as how much "bad conversation can corrupt a good life." (*I Cor. 15:33*)

Chapter 21 - Various texts from Solomon about depression.
Solomon the Wise wrote clearly on many occasions about the vice of sloth: "He who pursues idleness will be overwhelmed in poverty", (*Prov. 28:19*) both material and spiritual, for an idle person is bound to become the prey of different vices, and remain ever a stranger to the contemplation of God and to spiritual riches. Hence St Paul writes, "In Him you have become rich in all things, in all knowledge and wisdom". (*I Cor. 1:5*) We read elsewhere about the poverty of the idle, "The slothful man will be dressed in ragged robes and tatters". (*Prov. 23:21 LXX*) He will certainly not deserve to be dressed in those robes of incorruption of which the Apostle says, "Clothe yourselves in the Lord Jesus Christ," (*Rom. 13:14*) and again, "Clad in the breastplate of righteousness and charity". (*I Thess. 5:8*) The Lord also sent a prophecy of the same over Jerusalem, "Arise, Jerusalem, clothe yourselves in your garments of glory". (*Isaiah 52:1*) Anyone who is sunk in the sleep of accedia and sloth, prefers to the fruits of labour the rags of idleness, which he has torn from the fullness of the sacred Scriptures, gathering for himself not a garment of glory and splendour but a vile covering of shameful excuses. Those who are customarily sunk in such stupor refuse to support themselves by the work of their hands, in the way in which St Paul worked without ceasing, and urged us to do. They misuse the words of Scripture and

place a sort of veil over their idleness, citing the texts, "Work not for food that perishes, but for that which endures to eternal life", *(John 6:27)* and "my food is to do the will of my Father". *(John 4:34)* These texts are but rags torn from the seamless robe of the Gospel, stitched up to cover the nakedness and shame of our laziness, whereas if we would be warm and decent in the precious robe of perfect virtue we should imitate the wise woman in Proverbs who was dressed in courage and dignity, and worked for herself and her husband, because of which it says, "She is girded with courage and dignity, she rejoices to the end of her days". *(Prov. 31:25 LXX)* Solomon again points to the vice of idleness, saying, "The ways of those who do nothing are thick with thorns", *(Prov. 15:19 LXX)* that is with vices like those which the Apostle has described in the text already quoted as being bred by idleness. Again, "the idle man is always in want", (Prov. 13:4 LXX) and St Paul comments on this, "do not want the possessions of others." *(I Thess. 4:11)* Finally, "idleness teaches many evil things", *(Ecclus. 33:29)* which the Apostle clearly expounds in the text already quoted, "doing nothing but meddling". *(II Thess. 3:11)* He adds another piece of advice to the foregoing, "Apply yourselves to work, so that you may live tranquilly", *(I Thess. 4:11)* and furthermore, "that you may fulfil your own work, and may behave decently towards those outside, and covet the goods of no one". *(ibid.)* He orders that the diligent should keep aloof from those whom he convicts of being disorderly and rebellious, saying "withdraw yourselves from any brother who does not behave well in accordance with the Tradition which they had received from us". *(II Thess. 3:6)*

Chapter 22 - How the monks in Egypt work with their own hands not only to meet their own needs but also to assist those in prison.

The Fathers throughout Egypt have learned from these examples never to allow the monks, especially the younger ones, to be idle, but with a good heart to reap perfect patience and humility from their ceaseless labour. They do not accept anything from others for their sustenance, and what is more their labours suffice not only to entertain visiting pilgrim monks, but also to contribute a considerable amount of support and nourishment for those throughout Libya who are in need or are hungry, and for those languishing in prison in the various cities. By making these donations they consider they are offering a just and true sacrifice to the Lord out of the work of their own hands.

Chapter 23 - How it is idleness that has prevented monastic communities from existing in the West.
That is why in our own country we have not seen monastic houses founded with such success, since the monks do not depend on their own produce, and so do not survive for long. If sufficient provision is made for them from the charity of others, they become lazy and dissatisfied, and unable to remain for long in one place. Therefore the old Fathers in Egypt were of the opinion that only a single demon attacks a working monk, whereas an idle one is a prey to innumerable devils.

Chapter 24 - Of Abba Paul, who every year used to burn what he had made with his hands.
A worthy Father, Abba Paul, who lived in a vast solitude called Porphyrium, sustained himself on palm fruits and a small garden which gave him enough to support and feed himself, and had no other possibility of performing useful work, since his desert dwelling lay distant seven stages or more from towns or inhabited country, and the cost of transporting any goods he had made would be more than they could possibly be worth. He used to collect palm fronds and carefully make a daily amount of work as if he were to support himself thus. When his cave was quite blocked up with the products of a whole year's careful work, every year he would put it on the fire and burn it. By doing this he showed that a monk cannot remain happily in one place without manual labour, nor ever rise to perfect virtue, so that even when the necessities of life do not demand it, he should perform it simply for the purification of his heart, the control of his thoughts, perseverance in the cell and the defeat and overthrow of accedia itself.

Chapter 25 - The words which Abba Moses said to me on the cure of accedia.

When I first began to dwell in the desert, I confessed to Abba Moses, the most outstanding of all those holy men, saying that on the previous day I had been greatly troubled by the plague of depression, and that I could not be cured from it any other way than by running immediately to see Abba Paul. Abba Moses replied, "You have not cured yourself of it, but demonstrated that you are all the more subject to it. It would trouble you with far more difficulties if you were a fugitive deserter, once it sees you daunted by the struggle and in headlong flight. For the future when battle is joined, as long as you do not desert your cell, or sink into sleep, you can dissipate its first assaults at once, if you choose, or learn how to triumph over it by endurance in the conflict. It has been proved by experience that the attacks of accedia should not be avoided by flight, but resisted and overcome."

BOOK ELEVEN

Of the Spirit of Conceit

Chapter 1 - How the seventh bout is against Conceit, and of its nature.
Our seventh bout is against the spirit of conceit (which we may call empty boasting or vainglory); it takes many forms, it is changeable and elusive, so that it is scarcely possible for even the most discerning eyes not just to be wary of it but to see through it and master it.

Chapter 2 - How conceit strikes the monk not only through his physical nature but also in his spirituality.
It does not only strike a monk in his physical nature, as other vices do, but also in his spiritual, assaulting the mind with a more subtle poison. One who would not be taken in by the vices of the flesh can be all the more vulnerable to spiritual onset; the more difficult to detect, the more dangerous the attack. When the devil has tried him with all the other vices in open and obvious ways, and in every contest has been resisted by his firm stand, then he crawls weakly away, and the downcast fiend will later attack his conqueror less dangerously. This vice on the contrary may first assault the mind in a carnal manner, but if it is repulsed with a shield of rejection, it changes its style and character, being a spirit of wickedness in many forms, and under the guise of virtue makes an attempt at wounding the victor and slaying him.

Chapter 3 - How changeable and elusive conceit is.
Other vices and temptations can be described as having but one simple form, but this one has many styles, forms and variations, assaulting the warrior on all sides, and pressing round the victor. It tries to wound the soldier of Christ in his dress and his appearance, in his bearing, his voice and his work; in his vigils and fasting, in his prayer, his solitude, his reading and his study, in his silence and his

163

obedience, in his humility and in his endurance. Like a perilous rock concealed by the swelling sea, it wreaks a wretched and unforeseen wreck, on those who were sailing before a favourable breeze, and who neither anticipated it nor guarded against it.

Chapter 4 - How conceit attacks a monk both from right and left.
Now if we wish to proceed on the royal road, "with the armour of righteousness on our right and on our left", St Paul bids us pass "through good repute and bad, through slander and through praise". (*II Cor 6:7-8*) Wisely steered amidst the rolling seas of temptation, with the Spirit of the Lord blowing behind us, we may follow the course of virtue; but if we veer either to left or right we must be aware that we will soon strike on dangerous reefs. Solomon the Wise warns us, "Turn neither to the right nor to the left", (*Prov. 4:27 LXX*), that is be not complacent about your virtue, nor vaunt yourself on the success of your right spirit, neither tack to the left to be struck by the boom of vice, so that, as St Paul says, you may "boast of your own confusion". (*Phil. 3:19*) For if the Devil fails to beget vanity under the guise of shining and well-girt garments, he will attempt to instil it in squalid sordid rags. If he fails to cast someone down by his honours, he will trip him in his humiliations. If he is unable to make him boast of wisdom and eloquence, he will make him stumble with sober silence. If he fast publicly, he will be struck with vainglory. If he conceal his fasting through disdain of reputation, he will be brought down by the vice of complacency. If he avoids offering long prayers where his brethren can see him so as not to risk the taint of conceit, he will not escape the pangs of pride because of his having prayed in secret and no one being aware of the fact.

Chapter 5 - A simile to illustrate the nature of conceit
The elders have an apt way of describing the nature of this affliction, as being like an onion, in that when you peel off one skin another is found immediately underneath, and new skins are uncovered as often as you peel them off.

Chapter 6 - How conceit is not extinguished even through the advantage of solitude.

Conceit does not give up the pursuit of one who flees into the desert, away from the company of all men, for it may be for the sake of reputation. The more he shuns the whole world, the more fiercely he is attacked. Conceit tries to make one man proud because of his endurance of toil and hardship, another because he is swift to obey, another because he exceeds others in humility. One is tempted for his learning, another for his wide reading, another for his diligence in keeping vigil. This disease strikes precisely where a man's virtues lie, inflicting deadly wounds in the very areas where the prizes of life are won. The enemy lies in wait for those who are striving to follow the way of holiness and perfection, in the very path in which they are walking, and hides deceptive snares as the blessed David sang, "In the way in which I was walking they have hidden snares for me". (*Psalm 141/2:4*) In the very path of virtue in which we walk, heading for the "prize of our sublime calling", (*Phil. 3:14*) as we run forward, confident in our progress, we tumble headlong, the souls' feet caught in the snares of conceit. In the same way, if we are secure from defeat in the struggle against the foe, we are overcome by the very achievement of victory. Indeed, another way in which we are deceived is when we exceed the degree of self-control which is in our reach, for we shall fail to persevere in our path, brought down by our bodily weakness.

Chapter 7 - How if we defeat conceit, it will rise again to fight more fiercely.

All other vices dwindle as we overcome them, and day by day become weaker in defeat. They lose ground and opportunity, and cool down, or at least are more easily detected and avoided as the contrary virtues grow against them. But this one rises again from defeat more eager for the fight, and when you think it is extinct, it recovers from its death all the more lively. Other types of vice normally only attack those whom they might defeat, whereas this one presses hardest on its conquerors. The more successfully we elude it, the harder it assaults us through our very joy in victory. It is the subtly changeable nature of our foe, to bring down the soldier of Christ with his own weapons, when he could not have been defeated by those of his enemies.

Chapter 8 - How conceit does not decrease in the desert, nor with age.
As we have seen, other vices can be laid to rest by a good choice of habitation, where the objects of sin, its opportunities and occasions can be avoided, till the vice cools and dwindles; this one on the other hand follows the fugitive into the desert, is not excluded from any place, nor starved for want of external circumstance. It draws its strength precisely from the successful virtues of its victim. Other vices gradually decline and disappear as time passes, as we have described, but in this case long life, unless it is marked by ceaseless effort and wise discernment, is not only no cure, but even leads to piling up new occasions for conceit.

Chapter 9 - How conceit is more perilous when mingled with virtue.
Other disorders, when they are opposed by their opposite virtues, are engaged in the open like battle in the light of day, and can easily be overcome or avoided: this alone when it is entwined with virtues is far more dangerously deceptive to the unwary warrior, as if battle were joined in confusion, fighting in the thick of night.

Chapter 10 - The Cower case of King Hezekiah, and how he was brought down by an attack of vainglory.
Consider King Hezekiah of Judah, a man of great merit in every way, who finds approval in the record of Scripture: (*II Kings 18*) after many accounts of his virtues, we find him struck down by one attack of conceit, till he, at whose prayer was granted the destruction of one hundred and eighty thousand warriors of Assyria, laid low by an angel by night, was himself overcome by vain boasting. (*II Kings 19:15, 35*) To pass over his long record of good deeds, which would take too long to recount, I will mention just this: after the end of his life had been announced to him, and the day of his death was decreed by the Lord, through one single prayer he won an extension of fifteen years

of life, when the sun went back by ten degrees which it had already passed in its setting. Returning on its course again the shadow once more lay on the lines it would have to pass again, thus granting a second period of daylight to the whole world, which was an unprecedented miracle against the fixed laws of nature. (*II Kings 20*) But after such incredible signs, and such well documented virtues, hear what Scripture says about his subsequent fall: "In those days Hezekiah was sick even to death, and he prayed to the Lord who heard him, and gave him a sign," through the Prophet Isaiah, namely the one of the returning sun which we read about in the fourth Book of the Kingdoms. But "he did not return to the Lord according to the benefit he had received, for his heart grew proud and wrath arose against him, and against Judah and Jerusalem." He was humiliated later for his "pride of heart, both he and the inhabitants of Jerusalem, although the wrath of the Lord was not to come upon them in the days of King Hezekiah". (*II Chron. 32:24-6*) How destructive and weighty is this disease of pride! Such righteousness, such virtues, such faith and devotion, which had merited a change in the very nature and laws of the universe, lost by one act of pride! He might have felt the wrath of the Lord at once, and all his merits been lost in oblivion as if they had never been, had he not returned to humility and so pleased the Lord. So one who fell from such a summit of achievement thrust down by pride, could not ascend to the height he had lost except by climbing again the ladder of humility. Shall we look at another example of a similar fall?

Chapter 11 - The case of King Uzziah, overcome by the same affliction.
Uzziah, the great-grandfather of the king we have been speaking of, was praised in the Scripture account for everything he did, but after testimonies of his great virtues, and the innumerable feats which he deserved to achieve for his piety and faith, see how he was cast down in a moment of vainglory. "The name of Uzziah went forth", we are told, "because the Lord was at his side and strengthened him, and when he was in his strength his heart grew proud to his own

destruction, and he neglected the Lord his God". (*II Chron. 26:15-16*) Observe this second example of a terrible fall, and see how these two men had become so righteous and perfect, after their triumphs and victories. Thus you may see how dangerous the outcome of success may be, for those who cannot be daunted by opposition, are easily tripped up by prosperity if they are unwary. Those who escape the perils of battle and the threat of death, fall vanquished by their own trophies of victory.

Chapter 12 - Various texts against Vainglory
St Paul warns us, "Do not be eager for praise", (*Gal. 5:26*) and the Lord, in rebuking the Pharisees says, "How could you believe, you who accept praise from each other, and do not seek the glory which comes from God alone?" (*John 5:44*) The holy David also says threateningly, "God has scattered the bones of those who set out to please men". (*Psalm 52/3:6*)

Chapter 13 - The different manners in which Conceit strikes at the monk.
For those who are new to the life, and those who have progressed very little in virtue and wisdom, conceit puffs them up because of their voice, in that they sing psalms exquisitely, or because they are slim and good-looking, or because their family is rich or noble, or because they have spurned military honours. It goes on to persuade them that they could easily have gained rank and wealth (which in reality they probably could never have done) if only they had stayed in the world, and it inflates them with futile schemes of improbable things, and of things which they never had possessed, and makes them proud as if they had really given them up.

Chapter 14 - How Conceit suggests they might rise in the hierarchy.
Often it instils an ambition for Holy Orders and the priesthood or diaconate. If a monk has been chosen for ordination, it makes him imagine himself ministering with such piety and correctness that he can give an example of holiness to other priests, and winning many

souls not only by his manner of life but also in his teaching and preaching. Even one dwelling in the desert or in a cell is made to imagine himself travelling round different houses and monasteries, and converting many by the eloquence of his fantasy discourses.

Chapter 15 - How Conceit intoxicates the mind. (This division is not found in Migne)
The unhappy soul is manipulated by conceit in this way, as if it were dreaming in the deepest sleep, so that seduced by pleasant thoughts of this kind, and full of fancies, he is unable to notice present reality or the brothers he is with, while he is wrapt in the consideration of these products of his day-dreams as if they were real.

Chapter 16 - On one whom his superior discovered in his cell caught up in vain conceit.
I remember hearing, while I was living in the desert of Scete that a certain old man had arrived near the door of one of the brothers whom he was intending to visit, and heard him inside murmuring something, so stopped for a moment to hear what passage he was reading from Scripture, or reciting from memory as is customary. When the devout eavesdropper put his ear to the wall to hear more clearly, he discovered him so caught up by the spirit of conceit as to be imagining he was in church preaching to the people. When the waiting elder heard him come to a conclusion, and change roles to dismiss the catechumens like a deacon, he finally knocked on the door. The other came out, saw the elder, made the usual gesture of respect and brought him in. Once inside, being uneasy in his conscience about his fantasies, he asked if the elder had come to any harm through standing so long at the door. The old man replied pleasantly enough, with a smile, "I only arrived when you were dismissing the catechumens."

Chapter 17 - How vices cannot be cured except by detecting their origins and causes.
I thought it necessary to insert that passage to enable us to be aware

of how strong the attacks of this vice can be, and the manner in which the unhappy soul may be tormented by it, for we learn not only in theory but by examples as well, so as to avoid the snares and decoys which the enemy uses. The Egyptian Fathers without exception put themselves up as examples, and frankly admit and confess all their struggles against vice, whether suffered now or once suffered when they were younger, as if they were enduring them now, so that as they reveal how they have been deceived by all their own temptations, the younger monks who are listening to them may know the secrets of their struggles, and considering them may learn, as in a mirror, both the origins of the vices that trouble them, and their cure. Thus instructed before the event about future problems, they can explain how to anticipate them, confront them and defeat them. Like skilful doctors who do not only treat existing diseases, but know how to prevent future ones, and to take precautions with wise advice and medicine, in the same way these true doctors of the soul treat the emerging diseases of the heart in advance with their spiritual teaching like a heavenly antidote, and do not allow them to grow in the minds of the young ones, instructing them both in the causes of their present temptations, and the means to cure them.

Chapter 18 - How a monk should avoid women and bishops.
The consistent and still current teaching of the old Fathers (which I am embarrassed to repeat, I who failed to escape from my girl cousin, or elude the hands of the bishop) is that in all ways a monk should flee women and bishops. Neither would allow him, once entangled in their company, either to apply himself to peaceful work in his cell, or to cleave to divine contemplation, in the consideration of holy things with undistracted eye.

Chapter 19 - Remedies against the evil of conceit.
Now the athlete of Christ who yearns to compete aright in the true spiritual games, must not delay to defeat this manifold and varied monster in every way. We can escape it, when it assaults us on all sides

in its many forms with this remedy: remember the verse of David, "The Lord has scattered the bones of those who set out to please men". (*Psalm 52/3:6*) First of all we should not allow ourselves to do anything for the sake of conceit and in order to be praised. Then if we have made a good start at anything, we should try to keep at it with the same intention, otherwise all the fruits of our effort would be lost as conceit creeps in. We should carefully avoid anything in our behaviour towards our brothers that is or seems to be at all out of the ordinary, as something frivolous, and keep away from whatever might make us distinguished from others, and would make men praise us as if we were the only ones who ever did any work. These are the principal symptoms by which we can detect the deadly virus of conceit in ourselves: we can easily escape them if we remember firstly that we would lose all the benefit of our efforts if we did them with conceit in mind, and secondly, we would become liable to a severe accusation of being sacrilegious, and merit eternal suffering. For indeed we would be choosing, for the sake of men's approval, to perform work in God's despite, work which we should have been doing for His sake; in the sight of Him who knows all that is done in secret, we would be shown up as preferring men to God, and the glory of this world to God's glory.

BOOK TWELVE

Of the Spirit of Arrogant Pride

Chapter 1 - How our eighth contest is against the spirit of Arrogance, and what its nature is.

Our eighth and last contest is against the spirit of arrogance. This plague may well be the last vice to be attacked, and is treated last, but it is first in order of origin and occurrence. It is a savage monster, fiercer than all those described already, and particularly assaults the perfect, ravaging with its deadly fangs those who have already arrived at the height of virtue.

Chapter 2 - Of the two types of arrogance.

There are in fact two types: one which attacks holy and spiritual men, while the other entangles beginners and those still subject to the flesh. Both types of arrogance can make us proud in relationship both to God and to man, but the first relates particularly to our standing in the eyes of God, the second to our reputation among men. God willing, we shall speak of the latter towards the end of this book (*section XXIV*) to the best of our ability. Here I propose to say something of the first type, which as I said particularly assaults those who are perfect.

Chapter 3 - How arrogance takes away all virtues at once.

There is no other vice which so reduces all virtues to nothing, and despoils a man, stripping him of all holiness and righteousness, as does arrogance. Like a universal plague, which is not satisfied with crippling one limb or organ, but corrupts the whole body in its deadly infection, it attempts to cast down and destroy in utter ruin those who stand already on the peak of virtue. Other vices are satisfied with their own limits and goal, and, while they do some general damage, oppose one virtue in particular, and press hardest against that one alone. To understand what I mean more clearly, consider how gluttony, that is greed or the appetites of the stomach, corrupts one's ability of self-restraint, while lust assaults chastity, and wrath destroys patience. Often one who is addicted to one vice is not totally without other virtues, but fails only in that one virtue which lies subject to the attacks of its opposite vice, while being able to retain the other virtues at least in part. This vice of arrogance, however, once it gains possession of the unhappy man, is like a ruthless tyrant; first it takes the inner citadel of virtue, and then lays waste the whole city and destroys it. It throws down the high bulwarks of holiness, and lays them level with the dust of vice, leaving the subject soul no further illusion of freedom. The more prosperous its prey had been, the heavier the yoke of servitude it imposes, and with heartless cruelty it strips us of all virtue.

Chapter 4 - How it was pride that turned the Archangel Lucifer into the Devil.
To realise how dangerous the power of this tyrant can be, remember how that archangel, who was named Lucifer for his dazzling splendour and beauty, was thrown down from heaven for no other crime than this, and fell from the happy height of an angel's rank to the depths of Hell, once stricken by the dart of pride. If arrogance of heart could hurl down from heaven to earth one adorned with such a degree of virtue in such a position of power, we can see from the greatness of that fall how careful we must be, we who are subject to the frailty of the flesh. To shun this lethal virus we must learn how to detect the causes and origins of the peril. No sickness can be cured, no remedy prescribed for those who are suffering, unless we carefully examine and investigate the causes of the disease. Lucifer was adorned with divine radiance, and outshone the other powers of Heaven through the Creator's gift, but came to believe that the splendid wisdom and beautiful virtue, which God's grace had bestowed on him, was the result of his own natural ability, not a gift from God's goodness. Preening himself on this, as if he needed no divine help in maintaining his pure state, he considered himself equal to God, as if like God he

had no need of any other; overconfident in his freedom of will, he thought that would be enough to supply him with all he needed for perfect virtue and perpetual happiness. That single thought of his was the primal fall. Abandoned by God, whom he thought he could do without, he became at once unstable and chaotic, realised the weakness of his own nature, and lost the happiness which he had enjoyed as God's gift. Since he chose the "words of destruction", saying, "I will ascend to heaven", and the "deceitful tongue", with which he said of himself, "I will be like unto the Most High", and of Adam and Eve, "You shall be like gods", (*Gen. 3:5*) "therefore God will destroy him in the end, will uproot him, and he will depart from his dwelling place, and his root from the land of the living." Then the just, seeing his ruin, "will fear, and will laugh at him, saying", (as we could also appropriately say of those who think they can achieve any good without God's protection and aid) "See a man who has not made God his helper, but has hoped in the multitude of his riches, and become great in his own vanity." (*Psalm 51/2:6-9, and Isaiah 14:13-14 alternatim*)

Chapter 5 - How the seeds of all vices emerge from arrogance.
This is the origin of our first fall, the cause of man's first disobedience. Creeping back into the firstborn of mankind, through the one whom it had already cast down, pride engendered both the weakness and the occasion of all vice. Once Adam had come to believe that he could acquire the glory of godhead by his own free will and effort, he lost even that glory with which he had been endowed by the grace of the Creator.

Chapter 6 - How this vice of pride is the last to be engaged in battle, although it arises and originates first.
It can be clearly seen in many texts of Scripture that the vice of arrogance, while it may be the last in order of our conflicts, yet it is first of all in origin, and is the chief of all sins and crimes. Unlike other vices it does not only destroy the virtue opposite to itself, namely

humility, but is the bane of all virtues together. It does not only assail the mediocre or insignificant, but especially attacks the strong on their peak of achievement. The prophet says of this spirit, "it feeds on the elect". (*Hab. 1:16 LXX*) Hence the holy David, who was always so careful to keep hidden what was in his heart, openly proclaimed to the One from whom the secrets of the conscience cannot be hid, "O Lord, my heart is not proud, my eyes are not lifted up; I have not walked among the great nor among marvellous things too much for me, lest I feel shamed". (*Psalm 130/1:1-2*) and again, "He who acts proudly shall not live in the midst of my house". (*Psalm 100/1:7*) He was aware how difficult such vigilance is even for the perfect, and did not presume on his own abilities but prayed for the help of God that he might escape unscathed by the weapons of this enemy, in the words, "Let not the foot of arrogance come upon me." (*Psalm 35/6:12*) He was afraid lest he himself fall into what is said of the proud, "God opposes the proud", (*James 4:6*) and "Unclean before the Lord is every man who exalts his heart". (*Prov. 16:5 LXX*)

Chapter 7 - The evil of arrogance, which is rightly opposed by God Himself.
What a great evil arrogance is, for it needs to be opposed not by a mere angel, nor any virtue contrary to itself, but by God Himself! We must be aware that nowhere is it said of those entangled in other vices that they have God for their opponent, that God resists the gluttonous, fornicators, the wrathful and avaricious, but only that "he opposes the proud". (*James 4:6*) The other vices only recoil on the heads of those who commit them, or those who take part with them, affecting only other mortal men. This one truly pertains to God, and for this reason is fit to own Him for its special opponent.

Chapter 8 - How God extinguished the pride of the Devil by His own humility : some texts on this point.
God, the Creator and Redeemer of all, knowing that pride is the source and origin of evil, worked to heal opposites by opposites, so that what pride had overthrown might rise again through humility. For

Satan said, "I will arise to heaven", (*Isaiah 14:13*) but the Lord answered, "My soul is humbled to the earth". (*Psalm 43/4:25*) The former claimed, "I shall be like unto the Most High", (*Isaiah 14:14*) to be answered, "He was in the form of God, and emptied himself to assume the form of a slave. He humbled himself becoming obedient even unto death." (*Phil. 2:6-8*) To "I will exalt my throne above the stars of God", (*Isaiah 14:13*) comes the answer, "Learn from me, for I am gentle and humble of heart". (*Matth. 11:29*) Again, "I know no master, and I will not let Israel go", (*Exod. 5:2*) is matched by, "If I said that I did not know Him, I should be a liar, but I do know Him, and I keep His commands." (*John 8:55*) Says the enemy, "Mine are the rivers, it is I who made them", (*Ezech. 29:3 LXX*) but He answers, "I can make nothing by myself, it is my Father who abides in me who performs works." (*John 5:30, 14:10*) To his "Mine are all the kingdoms of the world and the glory thereof, and I give them to those I choose", (*Luke 4:6*) is replied "He was by nature rich, but made himself poor, so that we might become rich through his bounty." (*II Cor. 8:9*) Says the one, "As eggs that have been deserted are gathered up, so I gathered up the whole earth, and there was none to move a wing, nor to open its mouth and chirrup", (*Isaiah 10:14*) and the other answers, "I have become like a pelican in the wilderness, I have kept vigil and become like a sparrow alone on a housetop". (*Psalm 101/2:7-8*) The Devil claims, "I have dried up all the flowing streams as I passed over them", (*Isaiah 37:25*) but the Lord replies, "Can I not beseech my Father, and he will furnish me with more than twelve legions of angels?" (*Matth. 26:53*) If we examine the origin of our first fall, and the foundations of our salvation, by whom and how the former was brought upon us, the latter granted, how carefully must we flee that terrible virus of pride, learning from Satan's fall, and from Christ's example!

Chapter 9 - How we too may defeat arrogance.

It is possible for us to evade the clutches of this evil spirit if whenever we become aware that we have advanced in any virtue, we repeat what

St Paul says, "It is not I, but the grace of God within me; by the grace of God I am what I am", (*I Cor. 15:10*) and "it is God who enables us both to will and to perform our good desires". (*Phil. 2:13*) The Saviour Himself also says, "He who abides in me and I in him, he will bear much fruit; for without me you can achieve nothing." (*John 15:5*) Also, "Unless the Lord build the house, they labour in vain that build it. Unless the Lord keep guard over the city, in vain does the sentry keep watch". (*Psalm 126/7:1 LXX*) Again, "It is vain for you to rise before dawn", (*ibid, v.2*) and "Victory is not to the willing, nor to the swift, but to God who has mercy". (*Rom. 9:16*)

Chapter 10 - How no one can attain the perfection of virtue and the happiness that has been promised by his own efforts alone.

No one, who is still clothed in the flesh which wars against the spirit, however "willing or swift" he be, can display such an ideal will or effort that he can attain that prize of victory and trophy of pure integrity, unless he be protected by the mercy of God, and so be fit to arrive at his great desire, the goal for which he is running. "For every good gift, every perfect gift comes from above, descending from the Father of lights", (*James 1:17*) and "What do you have that you were not given? And if you have been given it, how can you boast as if it were not a gift?" (*I Cor. 4:7*)

Chapter 11 - The example of David, and the Good Thief, and on our own calling to make known the grace of God.

If we consider that robber, who for a single confession of faith was admitted into paradise, (*Luke 23:40*) we shall understand how he attained that happiness through no merits of his own achievement, but as a gift from the mercy of God. Or if we remember King David, whose two serious and weighty sins were annulled by one act of contrition, (*II Sam. 12:13*) here too we see that he did not earn the indulgence of such a great sin through the merits of his own works, but that the grace of God was more than abundant, who looked upon his true repentance and wiped out the burden of his sins after one word of genuine confession. Quite apart from the first principle of human calling and salvation, for we are saved not of ourselves, nor by our own works, as the Apostle teaches, but by the gift and grace of God, (*Ephes. 2:8-9*) we can clearly see how the height of perfection is granted "not to the willing, nor to the swift, but to God who has mercy". (*Rom. 9:16*) No merits of ours, neither effort nor work can compensate, but God makes us victorious over our vices; the application of our own will does not avail for us, while still in the flesh, to ascend the steep height of integrity, for it is itself in bonds. No corporal mortification, no contrition of heart is sufficient to achieve true chastity in the inner man, for bare human effort is incapable of obtaining such virtue, which is the birthright of angels alone, the currency of heaven, unless God assist. All good things flow from His grace, for it is He who has granted us such lasting happiness, and such great glory, through the immensity of his generosity to our feeble will after such brief and slight efforts.

Chapter 12 - That there is no toil which can compare with the happiness we are promised.
The whole length of our present life, if you compare it with the eternity of future glory, is nothing; all our sorrows disperse before the contemplation of such immense happiness, and dissipate to nothing like smoke, vanishing like sparks.

Chapter 13 - What the elders teach on the pursuit of purity.
It is appropriate here to recount in their own words what we learnt from the Fathers, that is those who have depicted the path of perfection and demonstrated it not merely in words but in their actions, possessing it in deed and strength of spirit. They have passed on their own experience and their example can be trusted. They tell us that we cannot be really purified from fleshly vice until we understand that all our efforts and toil are inadequate to reach such a goal. Nor could we hold onto it without God's merciful help; we have to learn this not just from the teaching we have been given, but through our own experience of effort and virtue. No matter how

many fasts, vigils or readings we employ, how much solitary remote toil we expend, whatever our industry or effort can merit, we are quite incapable of grasping the splendid and sublime prize of pure integrity. The divine gift is never made as a payment for our own work or for human effort, but is granted by God's mercy to those who long for it.

Chapter 14 - How God's help is given to those who strive.
I do not say this as if I were making human effort void, trying to dissuade anyone from a purpose of industrious work, in fact I observe that it is the consistent opinion of the Fathers, not just my own, that we cannot attain perfection without this effort; yet of itself, without the grace of God, it is incapable of bringing us to our goal. When we say that human effort cannot alone achieve perfection without God's help, we must also affirm that God's merciful grace is granted only to those who make some real effort, for, in St Paul's words, grace is given "to those who are willing and those who are swift", (*Rom. 9:16*) just as we sing in the eighty-eighth psalm in the person of God: "I have given my help to the strong, and I have raised up the chosen one of my people." (*Psalm 88/9:20*) Our Saviour also teaches that it is given to those who ask, it is opened to those who knock, and it is found by those who seek, (*Matth. 7:7*) but our asking, knocking and seeking are insufficient and we need the grace of God to grant what we ask, open where we knock and let us find what we seek. He is at hand, if only we offer him an act of goodwill to give Him a chance to grant us all these things. For He indeed desires and longs for our perfection and our salvation more than we do ourselves. That is why the holy David recognised that he could not, by his own efforts, attain the outcome of his labour and toil, and besought the Lord in constant prayer to guide his actions, saying, "Direct the works of our hands over us, direct the work of our hands", (*Psalm 89/90:17*) and again, "Strengthen, O God, what you have worked in us". (*Psalm 67/8:29*)

Chapter 15 - From whom we should learn the Way of Perfection.
Now if we desire to reach the totality of true virtue in very fact,

we should follow those masters and guides who have not just dreamed about it in empty phrases but are capable of teaching us and bringing us to what they have truly learnt by experience, showing us the sure path by which we might achieve that goal; those I mean who can be shown to have reached it through faith, and not through works. The purity of heart, which they had gained, conferred on them in particular a greater and greater recognition of how sin pressed on them. Their sorrow for sin grew daily within them, as their purity of soul increased, and they brought forth profound sighs from the heart, as they came to realise how they could never free themselves from the stains and scars of sin, which were branded upon them again and again by the slightest thoughts. Therefore they proclaimed that their hope of future bliss lay not in the merit of their works but in the mercy of God, claiming nothing for themselves in their examination of conscience in comparison with others, for they attributed everything to divine grace rather than their own efforts. They did not flatter themselves on the weakness and carelessness of lesser men, but paid more attention to those they knew had been really freed from sin and already attained eternal bliss in heaven; they gained a lasting humility, and by these considerations both avoided the peril of complacency and were never without material for aspiration and repentance. They knew full well that as long as they carried the burden of the flesh they would never arrive at that purity of heart for which they longed.

Chapter 16 - We cannot aspire to the work which brings perfection without the mercy and inspiration of God.
Now as we have learnt from the teaching of the Fathers, we should be eager for perfection, using fasting, vigils, prayers, mortification of heart and body, lest we lose all these things through the swelling of pride. It is not enough to believe ourselves incapable of reaching perfection through our own efforts and works, but we must know that we cannot even perform the very works which aim at perfection (i.e. our labour, toil and study) without the help of God's protection.

Through the grace of His inspiration, at His chiding, with His encouragement we can perform these works; and in His love He does pour that grace into our hearts, either through other people or by His direct intervention.

Chapter 17 - Various texts which show how we can do nothing towards our own salvation without the help of God.

Our Saviour has instructed us, in everything that we do, not only on what to think but also what to confess. "I cannot do anything of myself", he said, "but the Father who dwells in me, he does these works". *(John 5:30, 14:10)* Speaking in His nature as man, He says that He can do nothing of Himself; and we, dust and ashes that we are, think we can do without the help of God in matters pertaining to our salvation! Let us learn then, through our perception of our own feebleness and His aid in so many examples, to proclaim daily with the saints, "I was on the brink of falling, and the Lord upheld me. The Lord is my strength and my praise, He has become my saviour." *(Psalm 117/18:13-14)* "Unless the Lord assist me, my soul is on the point of dwelling in Hell. Though I used to say my foot has slipped, your mercy, O Lord, helped me. According to the multitude of woes in my heart, your consolations have made my soul rejoice." *(Psalm 93/4:17-19)* As we observe our hearts becoming stronger through the fear of the Lord and through patience, we can say, "The Lord has become my foundation, He has led me out into a wide place." *(Psalm 17/18:19-20)* As we understand our wisdom to grow through what we have achieved, we should say, "Since you light my lamp, O Lord my God, lighten my darkness; since by you I am delivered from temptation, in my God I will leap over the barrier." *(Psalm 17/18:29-30)* When we perceive that we have acquired some ability to endure, and are walking more easily and smoothly in the path of virtue, let us say, "O God, you gird me with strength, and lay a clear path before me, by you my feet are made swift as a hart's, and you set me on the heights; you instruct my hands in fighting." *(Psalm 17/18:33-5)* When we have learned discretion, and are thus capable of escaping our foes, let us proclaim to God, "Your training has corrected me for a purpose, your own instruction will teach me. You have enlarged my steps beneath me, and my footsteps are not unsteady." (*Psalm 17/18:36-7*) Once I am strengthened with your wisdom and power, I will advance towards the future with confidence, saying, "I will pursue my foes and overtake them, I will not turn aside until they are overthrown. I will wear them down, they will not stand; they will fall beneath my feet." (*Psalm 17/18:38-9*) Again, mindful of our weakness, and how without His aid we are incapable of overcoming those violent foes, the vices, clothed as we are with fragile flesh, we should say, "In your strength we shall scatter our enemies; in your name we shall repel those who arise against us. I will not hope in my bow, and my sword shall not save me, for you have saved us from those who oppress us, and you have confounded those who hate us." (*Psalm 43/4:6-8*) "You have girded me with strength for the battle, and have put beneath my feet all those who opposed me. You have made my enemies turn their backs on me, you have confounded those who hate me." (*Psalm 17/18:40-1*) Aware that it is not by our own weapons that we can conquer, we shall say, "Take up weapons and shield, arise to help me; draw your sword and engage those who persecute me; say to my soul, I am your salvation." (*Psalm 34/5:2-3*) "You have made my arms into a bronze bow, you have given me the protection of your salvation, your right hand sustained me." (*Psalm 17/18:35-6*) "For our fathers did not win this land with their own swords; it was not their arms that gave them victory, but your right hand, your arm, the light of your face, for you took delight in them." (*Psalm 43/4:4*) In short, running through all God's benefits, with thanksgiving in mind, thinking of the battles we have fought, the wisdom that has illuminated us, the training in discernment which we have received from Him, how His arms have taught us, and strengthened us with a girdle of virtue, how our enemies have turned their backs on us, and He has given us the strength to scatter them like dust before the wind, let us wholeheartedly cry unto Him, "I will love you, Lord, my strength; the Lord is my foundation and stronghold, my deliverer; my God is my helper, I will hope in Him; my protector and the horn of my salvation; He upholds me; I will call on the Lord with praise, and I will be saved from my foes." (*Psalm 17/18:2-4*)

Chapter 18 - How we are given strength by God's grace every day as well as in our nature.

We do not only give Him thanks for the reasons that He has created us with intelligence, endowed us with the power of freewill, poured upon us the grace of baptism, and granted us the knowledge and assistance of His law; but also because His daily care watches over us. He delivers us from the wiles of the enemy, co-operates with us in defeating the vices of the flesh, protects us from perils of which we are not aware; he guards us from falling into sin, aids us and enlightens us, so that we can recognise and acknowledge that He Himself is our helper (although some understand that this is the purpose of the Law). We give thanks too because at His secret prompting we feel vexed by our own sins and negligence; we are chastised for our benefit when He deigns to visit us; we are sometimes dragged by Him to safety against our inclination, and finally our own actual free will, which is so easily led to vice, is directed by Him to a better result, and He turns it by His inspiration towards the way of virtue.

Chapter 19 - How this doctrine on the Grace of God was handed down from the Fathers.

This is the humility we should have before God, this is the true faith of the first Fathers, which has remained unchanging among their successors until today. The miracles of the Apostles, which were so often manifest in them, bear undoubted witness to that faith, not only before us, but before unbelievers and the unfaithful. The Fathers kept the simple faith of the fishermen in a simple heart, and did not conceive it in worldly wisdom, through logical argument and Ciceronian eloquence. No, it was through living a blameless life, behaving sincerely, and by correcting their faults that they came to understand by the evidence of their own eyes how nature may be perfected in that same faith. Without this faith no one can understand devotion to God, the elimination of vice, the improvement of morals and the fullness of virtue.

Chapter 20 - Of one who was surrendered to a wicked spirit because of blasphemy.

I knew one of the monks - and would that I had not, since he has later allowed himself to be saddled with the same Holy Orders as myself! He confessed to one of the holy fathers that he was troubled with a serious temptation of the flesh, for he was consumed with an unbearable desire to be the passive partner rather than the active one in sins against nature. The confessor, being a true doctor of the soul, clearly discerned the inner reason and source of this affliction. He sighed deeply, saying, "The Lord would never have allowed you into the power of such a wicked spirit, had you not committed some blasphemy against him." The other, on this revelation, fell at once to the ground before his feet, full of admiration, realising that God had revealed the secrets of his heart, and confessed that he had indeed blasphemed with wicked thoughts against the Son of God. So we can see how one who is possessed by a spirit of pride, or who blasphemes against God, will be deprived of perfect virtue and fail to win the prize of chastity, for he has injured the One from whom the gift of purity should be expected.

Chapter 21 - The case of Joash, King of Judah, showing what his pride brought on him.

We read of something similar in Chronicles: Joash the King of Judah was brought to the throne by Joiada the High Priest at the age of seven, and was entirely praiseworthy, as Scripture tells us, as long as that celebrated priest lived. After the death of Joiada however, hear what Scripture says, and how he was puffed up with pride till he fell into base passions: "After Joiada died, the nobles of Judah came in to reverence the King. He was taken in by their flattery, and abandoned the Temple of the Lord the God of his fathers, to serve groves and graven images, till a great wrath arose against Judah and Jerusalem for this sin." (*II Chron. 24:17-18*) And a little later, "When the year came round, there came against him an army from Syria, which invaded Judah and Jerusalem, slew all the leading men of the people, and sent all the booty to the king in Damascus. And although it was only a small number of Syrians that came, the Lord gave into their hands an infinite multitude, because he had deserted the Lord the God of his fathers. Joash himself they treated with great indecency, and on their departure left him in deep distress." (*II Chron. 24:23-5*) Do you see how his pride brought him to be subject to sordid and criminal treatment? He was so swollen with pride that he allowed himself to be revered like God, and so was given over, as St Paul says, "to disgraceful lusts and wicked ways, to suffer things unseemly." (*Rom. 1:26, 28*) As Scripture says, "Every man who exalts his heart will be unclean in God's eyes." (*Prov. 16:5 LXX*) He who was puffed up with pride of heart, was given over to be the sport of vile practices, till he could be so humiliated, defiled in body and conscious of disgraceful lusts, as to realise how unclean he was, which in his pride of heart he had been unwilling to see. The humiliating treatment of his flesh made clear the secret uncleanness of his heart which the disease of pride has infected, and he was shown to be impure by the public abuse of his body because he would not acknowledge how unclean he was in the pride of his soul.

Chapter 22 - Every proud soul will be subject to abuse by wicked spirits.
By this we can clearly see how every soul which is possessed by the cancer of arrogance, is handed over to the Syrian intelligence, I mean to wicked spirits, and is entrapped in fleshly temptations, so that it may realise how impure and defiled it is at least in the earthy vices that humiliate it; for it was so lukewarm as to be incapable of understanding how impure its arrogance of heart had made it in the sight of God. Humiliated like this, one might recover from that early tepidity and be more eager and quick to apply oneself to spiritual improvement, once broken down and crushed by the shame of fleshly desires.

Chapter 23 - How perfection can never be gained except through humility.
Clearly then we must understand that no one can attain the goal of
perfect purity except through true humility. He should display this
first to his brethren, then to God in the secrecy of his heart, and
believe that without God's help granted him moment by moment, he
is quite incapable of obtaining the perfection he desires and for which
he so earnestly strives.

Chapter 24 - Who are affected by spiritual pride, and who by earthly.
That is enough for us to say, as far as our limited ability reaches, about
spiritual pride, which as we have seen, attacks those who are perfect.
That sort of arrogance is unknown to the majority and beyond their
experience, for there are not many who attempt to win perfect purity
of heart and so qualify for that level of contest, and few have been
really healed of the preceding vices which we have already described,
book by book, along with their cures. Spiritual pride only assaults
those who have conquered the earlier vices and are already on the
point of reaching the summit of virtue. Since the sly foe is unable to
overcome them in fleshly faults, it tries to overthrow them and
undermine them in spiritual ruin. In this way it attempts to rob them
of all the merits of their earlier service which they had gained with so
much effort. We however, who are still entangled in earthly passions,
are not fit to be tempted in this way, but in a more basic way we are
undermined by the joy of the flesh, so to speak. That is why I think
I should keep my promise to say something about this sort of pride
which particularly attacks us and men like us, and is most likely to
trouble the minds of young men and beginners.

Chapter 25 - A description of fleshly pride, and what evils it begets in a monk.
Now what I have called fleshly pride settles on a monk if he has made
a tepid and ill-instructed beginning to his monastic life; it does not
allow him to descend to true Christian humility from his original
worldly status, but begins by making him disobedient and rude. It
does not let him become gentle and affable, nor be at ease with his

brethren in the common life; nor can he rid himself of earthly wealth and give it up as our God and Saviour bade. Since monastic life is nothing other than the profession of self-denial and the Cross, it cannot be based or stand on any other foundation, but a monk must understand that he is spiritually cut off from the activities of this world, and also remember daily that his body must die. Pride on the other hand makes him hope for long life, reminds him of many complicated infirmities, and causes confusion and shame. If he renounces his goods and begins to live on the support of others, not his own, pride suggests that it would be much better to find his food and clothing from his own resources, presuming to quote a text we have already commented on, but some are incapable of understanding through the sluggish meanness of their hearts; namely, "It is more blessed to give than to receive." (*Acts. 20:35; see above, Book 10, section XVIII*)

Chapter 26 - How one who has made a bad beginning steadily degenerates to a worse condition.
Once a monk is obsessed with this anxiety, and by devilish doubt deflected from the spark of faith (which seemed to have been enkindled when he was first converted), he will begin to collect up carefully the money he had formerly begun to disperse, and to hoard it all the more greedily as if it could not be recovered once spent. A worse outcome is to claim back what he had originally given away; worse still to accumulate more than he had before, which is the last stage of corruption. All that remains of his renunciation of the world is the bare name and title of monk. Once that foundation of evil and vice is laid, the whole edifice of sin is bound to arise, for nothing could be erected on such rotten foundations except the tragic ruin of a miserable life.

Chapter 27 - A description of the vices which are engendered by pride.
When the mind is hardened by these passions, it begins in base tepidity, and inevitably decays from day to day, bringing its remaining life to a wretched end. Taking delight in crude desires, it is overthrown

by what St Paul calls unholy greed, for his verdict on it is "servitude to fetishes and idols", (*Col. 3:5*) and, "The root of all evil is the love of money." (*I Tim. 6:10*) We can never admit true and single-minded Christian humility into the heart if we boast of noble birth; or swagger about worldly prestige, gained by the body, not the mind; or exalt in wealth accumulated for our ruin, which makes us unhappy to bear the discipline of the monastery or to learn from the teaching of the elders. Once someone has been infected with the virus of arrogance, he is not only unwilling to keep any rule of submissive obedience, but will not even listen to the teaching of perfection. He conceives in his heart so great a dislike of spiritual conversation that if by any chance such a discussion arise, he is quite incapable of staying still to listen, but gazes stupidly around the place and is always looking askance in another direction. Instead of devout sighs, his dry throat generates phlegm, and he is continually coughing. He twiddles his fingers, and makes writing or painting gestures with them. He shifts his whole body from side to side, so that while the spiritual discourse proceeds, you might think he was in agony from itching fleas or chronic piles.

However straightforward the discourse be for the benefit of the audience, he imagines it to be aimed at himself as an insult. As long as the spiritual life is under consideration, he is so taken up with his own resentment that he does not think of what he might retain for his own benefit, but spends his energies in wondering why each point had been made, or considering inwardly how he could oppose them. None of the salutary instruction can he take to heart, or find any profit in it. Thus it happens that spiritual discourses are useless to him, in fact they are destructive, since for him they are an occasion of greater sin. As long as he thinks the whole thing is directed against him, he is more and more hardened in his obstinacy, and more provoked to anger. Eventually he raises his voice, speaks abruptly, replies in bitter confusion, and walks out haughtily. Now he is quick to speak, long winded indeed, never happy in silence except to brood privately some bitterness against his brother; his silence betokens not repentance nor the slightest humility, but pride and indignation, until you would be hard put to it to decide which is worse, his volatile and touchy cheerfulness or his sullen and acidic silence. When he speaks it is out of turn, making fatuous jokes, in random uncontrolled frivolity; his silence is full of anger and bitterness, and maintained solely in order to prolong as long as possible the grievance against his brother which he is tacitly incubating, so far from demonstrating the virtue of patient humility. Being eaten up with this cancer, he easily depresses everyone else, and is too proud to humiliate himself and so ease his brother's pain. If the other offer him apology, he rejects it with scorn. He is not touched or softened by his brother's apology; on the contrary he is all the more indignant in being anticipated by the other's humility. Thus even humble apology and conciliation, which would normally put an end to this devilish temptation, can become a cause of greater ire.

Chapter 28 - On the pride of a certain brother.
I have heard of a local case, which is horrifying to relate; a young monk was rebuked by his abbot for abandoning the humility which he had briefly practised on his first profession, and for being enflamed with devilish pride. He replied indignantly, "Do you think I put up with being humiliated for a period in order to be a junior all my life?" The elder was so amazed at this brash and uncouth reply, that his whole train of speech was interrupted, as if these words had been spoken by Lucifer of old, not by a mortal man. He was unable to utter a word against this arrogance, but only heartfelt groans and sighs; while he pondered silently within himself what is said of our Saviour, "He was in the form of God, and humbled himself to become obedient", not for a period as the other had said in his diabolical spirit of pride, but "even unto death." (*Phil. 2:6, 8*)

Chapter 29 - Indications to detect fleshly pride in a soul.
To pass briefly over what has been said of this type of arrogance, we shall do what we can to put together the symptoms, so that those who yearn to know about perfection may recognise its marks in the external

behaviour of a man. I think a few things need to be repeated, so that we can be clearer what symptoms will help us detect and diagnose it, and where the exposed roots are, the visible causes of this infection, which may be seen and examined and thus more easily eliminated or avoided. This deadly disease can be reduced to health when early observation enables measures to be taken against its dangerous fevers and perilous attacks while they are still beginning. If we detect its first onset, we can wisely anticipate it with thoughtful precautions. So, as I have said, the inner state of a man can be detected from his external behaviour, and these are the symptoms (already listed) which indicate the pride of the flesh: first the patient is brash when he talks, sullen when he does not, elated and overwhelming when he is cheerful, unreasonably gloomy when he is depressed. He is bitter when questioned, glib when talkative, prolific in verbiage without any profound consideration. He knows nothing of patience, and is a stranger to charity, bold in inviting arguments, but feeble in defending himself. He is slow to obey except where his own preference and will are in agreement, disagreeable when receiving correction, soft at restraining his own desires, but finds it hard to submit to others; he always wants to make his own terms, and is never prepared to give in to what others want. In short, he is incapable of listening to advice that might save him, but in all matters prefers his own judgement to that of his superior.

Chapter 30 - How one rendered tepid by his pride longs to be set in charge of others.

Once a man has been led down these steps by his obsessive pride, he begins to find the discipline of the monastery abhorrent, so that, as if he were drawn away from the fellowship of the brothers by his own perfection, and kept away from the benefit of tolerant humility by the vice and inconvenience of others, he longs to dwell in a cell alone, or indeed to found a monastery as if he could attract several others, and is eager to collect people to teach and train. Thus a bad disciple becomes a worse master. With this haughty spirit he plunges into disastrous decline and calamity, becoming neither a real monk nor a real secular. What is worse, he still promises himself a state of perfection in such a wretched way of life.

Chapter 31 - How we may overthrow pride and attain to perfection.
Now if we want to see on our construction the arising of pinnacles which are perfect and pleasing to God, we must be sure to lay the foundations not as our will and desires dictate, but according to the strict discipline of the Gospel. These foundations can be nothing other than the fear of God, and humility, which emerge from a mild and simple heart. Humility cannot be acquired except through detachment from possessions; if we have lost sight of that, we cannot hope to take hold of the desired obedience, strong endurance, peaceful tranquillity or perfect charity. Without those, our hearts are incapable of becoming the dwelling place of the Holy Spirit, as the Lord says through the prophet: "On whom will My spirit rest, except on the humble, the peaceful, the one who fears my words?" (*Isaiah 66:2*) - or, as the versions more faithful to the Hebrew have it, "to whom shall I look except to the poor, the contrite of spirit, the one who fears my words?"

Chapter 32 - How pride, which robs us of all virtues, can be extinguished by true humility.
Because of this, the athlete of Christ, who desires to be crowned by the Lord after completing the legitimate spiritual competition, must be quick to eliminate this savage beast which devours all virtue. He must know that as long as it lurks in his breast he will not only be unable to rid himself of vices of all kinds, but also any virtues he may seem to have will perish through its poison. The edifice of virtue cannot arise in the soul except on foundations of true humility laid in our hearts. Firmly rooted, they will be strong enough to support a tower of perfect charity. As we have seen, the first course must be to exhibit real humility towards our own brethren in the depths of our hearts, never allowing ourselves to cause them grief or hurt them; this we

could not possibly do except by real detachment, consisting in renouncing all our property and practising poverty, and the love of Christ will lay this foundation in us. Next we must take on the yoke of obedience, in a simple submissive heart with no pretence, so that no will remains in us except to do the abbot's command. That cannot be achieved other than by one who considers himself dead to this world, to the extent of thinking he is too inexperienced to make decisions, so that he accepts whatever his superiors decree without any argument, believing these commands to be sacred and given to him by God.

Chapter 33 - The remedy against the plague of Pride.
Once we have brought ourselves to this point, there will surely follow a truly peaceful and undisturbed state of humility, so that we can consider ourselves inferior to others, and cheerfully accept whatever is asked of us, however burdensome, depressing or injurious, because our superiors require it. Such commands will be readily accepted by us and considered to be trivial or no burden at all, if we carefully recollect the Passion of Our Lord and the saints, thinking how much lighter our own sufferings are and how far removed we are from their merits and behaviour. We should also consider how soon we are to leave this world, and how we shall shortly be their companions, at the end of this brief life. Such a consideration is fatal to pride, and indeed to every type of vice. After that we shall display the same degree of humility towards God. That will enable us to recognise that we can achieve nothing of ourselves towards the goal of perfection, without His enabling grace. Truly we shall believe the very fact that we can understand this to be His gift as well!

Subscribers to the HONEYCOMB SERIES

*The Saint Austin Press gratefully acknowledges the support of
the following individuals who have made possible the
publication of this edition by their subscription.*

Rev. R.W. Hugh Allen, Coity, Bridgend.
Rev. C.W. Baker, Chatham, Kent.
Dr. G.J. Berry, Woodhall Spa, Lincolnshire.
Mr. Robert Binyon, London.
Rev. S.D. Brown, Leeds.
Rev. Christopher Connor, Edgware, Middlesex.
Mrs. J. Curtin, Helston, Cornwall.
Mr. Michael J. Doolan, Tremorfa, Cardiff.
Mr. Ray Duffy, Meols Wirrall, Merseyside.
Dr. M.D.E. Evans, Burghclere, nr. Newbury, Berkshire.
Mr. Lionel Gracey, Sunningdale, Berkshire.
Mr. George Grynowski, Raimals, Wellingborough, Northamptonshire.
Rev. Michael W. Hawkins, Pleasantville, Nova Scotia.
Mr. G.E. Hester, St. Ambrose College, Altringham, Cheshire.
Mr. Kevin Hickey, Church Accrington, Lancashire.
Fr. James B. Hurley, Wimbledon, London.
Professor Paul Jackson, University of Reading.
Mr. Neville McNally, Southsea, Hampshire.
Mr. Peter Molony, Great Elm, Somerset.
Miss Janet Boyd Moss, Edinburgh.
Mr. Daniel Moylan, London.
Mr. D.W. Newcombe, Shorne, Gravesend, Kent.
Mr. Christopher Newton, Ripe, East Sussex.
Mr. V.G. Osborn, Leicester.
Mr. J.V. Parker, Leicester.
Mr. Michael Parsons, Newton Abbott, Devon.
Mr. J.C. Petrie, Orrell, Wigan, Lancashire.
Mr. G.J. Pinsard, Saint Sampson's, Guernsey.
Mr. Michael Price, Manselton, Swansea.
Mr. Peter Pryer, Church Crookham, Fleet, Hampshire.
Rev. Roman Przetak, Lower Bullingham, Hereford.
Mr. Christopher K. Rance, Dulwich, London.
Rev. Scott M. P. Reid, Willesden, London.
Mr. John A. Richards, Orton Wistow, Peterborough.
Mr. David J. Scorey, Cheadle, Staffordshire.
Mr. Anthony F. Schmitz, Aberdeen.
Dr. Margaret Sealey, Shirley, Solihull.
Miss I.H.S. Shaw, Port Navas, Falmouth, Cornwall.
Mr. G.V. Shugg, London.
Mr. J. Smiles, Brewood, Staffordshire.
Mr. P.A.H. Thomas, K.S., Eton College, Eton, Berkshire.
Mrs. Leslie von Goetz, Newport-on-Tay, Fife.
Fr. Eric Wright, Chelsea, London.
Fr. William Young, Barking, Essex.

THE HONEYCOMB SERIES

The Saint Austin Press is now accepting subscriptions for its eagerly awaited HONEYCOMB SERIES. The aim of the series is to provide sound spiritual reading for lay people, priests and religious by publishing long out of print or previously unpublished spiritual classics such as St John Cassian's "The Monastic Institutes", or Blosius' "Comfort for the Faint Hearted."

Each book in the Series will be uniform with the present volume: quality cloth hardcovers, with properly sewn pages, headbands and ribbon, together with a beautiful dustjacket featuring an appropriate reproduction of a religious painting.

Subscribers are invited to sign up for the first five books in the HONEYCOMB SERIES at a cost of £60 (£70 overseas). Future works in the series include further writings by Cassian and Blosius as well as works by Fray Juan de los Angelos, the spiritual mentor to St John of the Cross. A panel of editorial advisors chaired by the series editor, Fr Jerome Bertram, is suggesting and selecting suitable texts, which will be edited, translated and submitted for *Nihil Obstat* and *Imprimatur*. The books will appear every four to six months.

As a mark of our gratitude for their support of the HONEYCOMB SERIES subscribers will be acknowledged by name at the back of each of the five editions to which they subscribe. We have chosen the name 'HONEYCOMB' to represent the noble industry of the bee, which can be seen as a type of the Christian scholar, collecting wisdom from Scripture and from the Fathers and Doctors, as a bee collects nectar from many different flowers.

To enter your name as a subscriber to the HONEYCOMB SERIES and receive the next five titles as soon as they are published, simply send a note of your name and address together with payment for £60 (£70 for overseas customers) to :

The Saint Austin Press, 296 Brockley Road, London, SE4 2RA

Second title in the HONEYCOMB SERIES • Publication: April 1999

COMFORT FOR THE FAINT-HEARTED
by Ludovicius Blosius (Louis de Blois)
ISBN 1 901157 09 1

This little book, written half a millennium ago, offers present day humanity what it so desperately yearns for: reassurance that God loves it. How many of our contemporaries have lost hope, both in God and in each other! It is all too easy to look at the world around us and come to the depressing conclusion that everything is getting worse and worse, and that God, if there is a God, simply does not care.

When Blosius wrote this book in 1555, his world was torn by new religious divisions and on the brink of annihiliation by the Turks. The new divisions and hatreds within Christendom were abhorrent partly because they weakened the Christian west at the very moment when the threat from outside seemed greatest.

But the divisions were tragic enough in their own right. In an amazingly short space of time half of Europe was savagely cut off from the mainstream of Catholic Christianity, and barriers set up which show no signs of weakening even now. Consider that, along with the economic collapse, and the ever more tyrannical absolute monarchs who were establishing their nation-states in the wreckage of the Empire, and you can see that the first half of the sixteenth century was not a very comfortable time to live.

Blosius makes no mention of the problems of his age at all. He sets out to speak nothing but words of encouragement, to make his readers cheer up, persevere, find hope in God. Above all, he proclaims to them the unconditional love of God, who - he tells us over and over again - is on our side. He is not against us. He wills all men to be saved, and works ceaseless miracles to ensure that we are saved. Our sins and failures - though we must abhor them and repent them - are so insignificant in comparison that they are burnt up in the fire of God's love in less time than it takes for us to utter a prayer of sorrow, of hope, of love.

Blosius' advice, drawn from many eminent Christian teachers of the Middle Ages and the Rennaissance, is particularly timely for modern man, who now faces temptations towards indifference or desolation quite similar to those of his sixteenth century counterparts. The "still, small voice of calm" which is the orthodox Catholic message of the love of God is the voice which will still be heard when all the others have died away.

The Saint Austin Press' Titles

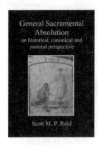

GENERAL SACRAMENTAL ABSOLUTION
Scott M. P. Reid
In this scholarly account, Reid argues that the use of General Absolution is not an appropriate response to the decline in confessions. A wide-ranging historical, canonical and pastoral perspective.

40 pages, paperback - stapled, £1.95 ISBN 1-901157-65-2

LIFE OF ST. EDWARD THE CONFESSOR
St. Aelred of Rievaulx
Translated into English for the first time by Fr Jerome Bertram, FSA. St. Edward built Westminster Abbey and was a great friend of the poor. An inspiring account of the life and miracles of England's Saintly King.

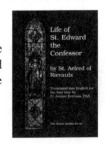

138 pages, paperback, £9.95, ISBN 1-901157-75-X

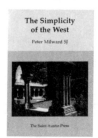

THE SIMPLICITY OF THE WEST
Peter Milward, S.J.
This work charts the idea of simplicity - as seen in the context of nature and tradition - through Socrates, St. Francis, St. Thomas Aquinas, to the present day. An exhilarating tour of Christian civilization with a profound message.

95 pages, paperback, £9.95, ISBN 1-901157-95-4

A BITTER TRIAL
Evelyn Waugh and John Carmel Cardinal Heenan on the Liturgical Changes *(Ed. Scott M. P. Reid)*
For the last decade of his life, Waugh experienced the changes being made to the Church's liturgy as "a bitter trial." In Heenan he found a sympathetic pastor and kindred spirit. This volume contains the previously unpublished correspondence between these prominent Catholics, revealing in both an incisive disquiet.

71 pages, paperback, £3.95, ISBN 1-901157-05-9

The Saint Austin Press' Titles

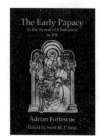

THE EARLY PAPACY
to the Council of Chalcedon in 451
Adrian Fortescue
A clear exposition and sound defence of the belief in the role of the Pope in the Church, drawing upon evidence from the Church Fathers up to 451 AD.

96 pages, paperback, £7.95, ISBN 1-901157-60-1

THE FACE OF THE NAZARENE
Noel Trimming
This dramatic and involving story is also a profound meditation on the Lord of the Millennia; Jesus Christ, the same yesterday, today and forever. It charts the impact of Christ on some of the people who knew him, in the hectic circumstances of their everyday lives.
157 pages, paperback, £9.95, ISBN 1-901157-90-3

NEWMAN'S MARIOLOGY
Michael Perrott
A study of the development of Newman's beliefs about Our Lady, from the staid "Anglican red-letter days" of his time in Littlemore to the intimate and inspiring poetry of "The Dream of Gerontius" and his "Meditations and Devotions." Scholary but immensely readable.
104 pages, paperback, £8.95, ISBN 1-901157-45-8

THE CATHOLICISM OF SHAKSPEARE'S PLAYS
Peter Milward, S.J.
The local tradition in Stratford is that Shakespeare "died a Papist." Professor Peter Milward, of Sophia University, Tokyo, argues that the whole of Shakespeare's work reveals a common thread of sympathy with the plight of persecuted Catholics under Queen Elizabeth and King James I.
144 pages, paperback, £7.95, ISBN 1-901157-10-5

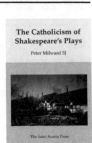

The Saint Austin Press' Titles

A VICTORIAN CONVERT QUINTET
Rev. Michael Clifton

In this fascinating study of the faith journeys of five converts to Catholicism from the Oxford Movement, Fr. Michael Clifton invites the reader to consider the lessons we might learn from this *Quintet* of learned men.

212 pages, paperback, £9.95, ISBN 1-901157-03-2

DARKNESS VISIBLE
A Christian Appraisal of Freemasonry
Rev. Walton Hannah

Addresses the question of whether involvement with Freemasonry is compatible with one's duty as a practising Christian. It includes the entire and authentic text of the Masonic ritual of the first three degrees and of the Royal Arch.

232 pages, paperback, £12.95, ISBN 1-901157-70-9

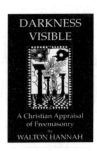

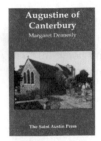

AUGUSTINE OF CANTERBURY
Margaret Deanesly

This study deals with St. Augustine's training, character and background; the origins of his mission; his work in Kent; the structure of the church he established; the nature of the ministry he founded for the continuance of his work.

175 pages, paperback, £12.95, ISBN 1-901157-25-3

CATENA AUREA
A Commentary on the Four Gospels
St. Thomas Aquinas

Drawing completely on the Church Fathers, St. Thomas provides an indispensable verse by verse commentary on the Gospels. Translated under Cardinal Newman, introduced by Aidan Nichols OP.

2,825 pages, hardback, 4-volume set, £85, ISBN 1-901157-40-7

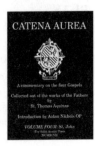

The Saint Austin Press' Titles

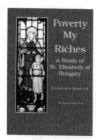

POVERTY MY RICHES
A Life of St. Elizabeth of Hungary
Sr Elizabeth Ruth Obbard ODC
An inspiring account of the thirteenth-century wife, mother and queen who endured suffering all her life and died among the poor and sick whom she loved so much. A woman's account of this life of extraordinary sanctity.
106 pages, paperback, £9.95, ISBN 1-901157-80-6

THE VENERATION AND ADMINISTRATION OF THE EUCHARIST
The Proceedings of the 1996 Second International Colloquium on the Liturgy, organised by the Centre International d'Études Liturgiques (CIEL).
Includes papers from leading theologians and explores aspects of the traditional Latin liturgy and the development of the Church's Eucharistic teaching.
255 pages, paperback, £12.95, ISBN 1-901157-15-6

ALTAR AND SACRIFICE
The Proceedings of the 1997 Third International Colloquium of historical, canonical and theological studies on the Roman Catholic Liturgy, organised by the Centre International d'Études Liturgiques (CIEL).
An inspirational and fascinating collection of academic papers on the traditional Roman Liturgy given by international experts.
192 pages, paperback, £12.95, ISBN 1-901157-85-7

THE CEREMONIES OF THE ROMAN RITE DESCRIBED
Adrian Fortescue & J.B.O'Connell
A reprint of the 1962 edition of this classic ceremonial manual for the traditional Latin Mass. Published to support the work of the new traditional religious communities in union with the Holy See.
424 pages, hardback, £24.95, ISBN 1-901157-00-8

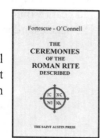

THE THREE YS MEN

Joseph Pearce

In his first novel, the author of the best-selling biography of Chesterton, *Wisdom and Innocence*, undertakes a journey through Sussex in the company of three myterious ghosts. These are Yore, the Ghost of Sussex Past (the thinly disguised ghost of Hilaire Belloc); Yo the Ghost of Sussex Present; and Yet, the Ghost of Sussex Future. En Route, the three spirits have many misadventures and can seldom agree on anything, constantly arguinging about the relative merits of tradition and modernity in relation to time and eternity.There is also a suprise appearance of Tim, the Ghost of Time Uncompleted (the thinly disguised Ghost of HG Wells). The final chapter adds several twists to the tale.

176 pages, hardback, £13.95, ISBN 1-901157-02-4

THE INVISIBLE CROWN

Michael McGrade

Amongst the Glorious litany of Catholic saints, who has heard of Nicholas and Dorothy von Flüe? Yet this fourteenth century couple united Switzerland and in so doing, surely saved Western Europe from the entrenchment of a fratricidal enclave to rival the Balkans. This fascinating and compelling story unveils one of the best kept secrets of Catholic Europe and bears a timely message for our tormented age.

152 pages, hardback, £14.95, ISBN 1-901157-76-8